Foreword by Marie Diam
of ATL Europe, Tea

TRANSFORMATION
LESSONS

38 Insights to Manifest
Your Best Life

ATL EUROPE

Transformation Lessons

First published in 2018 by

Panoma Press Ltd
48 St Vincent Drive, St Albans, Herts, AL1 5SJ, UK
info@panomapress.com
www.panomapress.com

Book layout by Neil Coe.

Printed on acid-free paper from managed forests.

ISBN 978-1-784521-49-3

FOREWORD

Marie Diamond
Founder and President of ATL Europe
Teacher from *The Secret*

Hello dear reader

You picked up this book in a bookstore or library, or perhaps bought it on Amazon, or received it as a gift. I do not know why you are reading this now, but I know there is no mistake in the universe. So perhaps you are in need of some of the wonderful stories and transformation lessons shared in this book. Maybe it means that you are somewhere stuck in your life, or you've lost courage, feel depressed or down and so possibly need some positive inspiration to get you out of this negative thought process or downward-spiralling part of your life. Perhaps you just need an inspiring evening story or a transformation lesson to help to start your day.

As one of the teachers in the hit movie and bestseller *The Secret*, I know how the 'law of attraction' works. I am sure you have asked God/the universe to attract money, success and love. Now you can use it to attract transformation and positive change in your life and to grow as a human being. Your soul needs more than physical and emotional needs. Your soul is here to help you find your purpose.

When I started ATL Europe, my vision was to attract transformational leaders to create a positive change in Europe and the world. I am so delighted that many amazing co-authors have responded to my call to create this book and to support you.

All the co-authors in this book, have found their purpose and are living it with intention. They are here to transform you, your families and your business, in Europe and throughout the world.

And to make change happen, you will need guidance. I hope that this book will support you in manifesting a positive transformation in your life. A good way to use this book is to ask, with intention, for an answer to a question. Then ask your soul to guide you to open this book for an answer. The story that you will read will help you. It is possible that the tool, the insight and even the author will inspire you to take the next steps. Feel free to check the websites of the different co-authors to learn about their transformational programs, tools and insights. Many of them have free gifts on their sites to support you even further on your transformational journey.

Maybe the book chose you to become part of the vision of ATL Europe to bring forth an enlightened Europe and world: you can do this by following the authors on social media. Perhaps you are a transformational coach, mentor, teacher, speaker, author or businessperson, and wish to be part of the ATL Europe membership. Let us know. Get in touch with us at www.atl-europe. org.

Pay the transformation forward by buying a second book or share this book after reading it yourself and give it to a person who needs positive change. Be part of the transformational movement we are creating in Europe and throughout the world.

With love

Marie Diamond

www.MarieDiamond.com

CONTENTS

INTRODUCTION

This book, *Transformation Lessons, 38 Insights to Manifest Your Best Life*, is a project of the Association of Transformational Leaders of Europe (ATL Europe).

ATL Europe is a heart-based community of transformational leaders seeking to bring about an enlightened Europe.

Transformational speakers, authors, teachers and businesspeople in European countries are members. The idea of starting this organisation was put forward by Marie Diamond. As a founding member of the Transformational Leadership Council created by Jack Canfield, she was inspired to create this non-profit organisation for European transformational leaders.

Owing to the nature of our work and extensive travel, we meet online and twice a year the members come together to take time to support one another as peers in becoming better transformational leaders and creating more impact with our work. We share our latest insights, tools and procedures and create a transformational family that we can count on, when we need, personally and in business.

Since 2012, our members have joined from the United Kingdom, Belgium, the Netherlands, Norway, Denmark, Iceland, Sweden, France, Spain, Austria, Germany, the Czech Republic, Slovakia, Cyprus, Croatia, Serbia, Greece, Poland, Slovenia and Monaco.

The idea of this book was born in April 2018, at an ATL Europe meeting in Florence, where the members were focused on renaissance. There is so much combined transformation potential in ATL Europe and we wish to share this with you, to inspire you in your personal transformation journey and to enlighten people in Europe and beyond to create individual and collective transformation.

As transformational leaders, we have all been through our own process of inner change. Some of us had to overcome deep fears, all sorts of abuse, a train accident, near death, bankruptcy, alcoholism, exhaustion, immune diseases, eating disorders, being bullied, divorce, and much more. But through a process of transformation and being guided by transformational authors, teachers, coaches and mentors, we were lifted up and inspired to rise above all this. We started sharing our stories, making it our passion to share details of our transformation and even to make a living out of this.

After the Florence meeting, two daughters of ATL Europe members launched ATL Junior. These teenagers are also sharing transformational lessons in this book. They are the future of Europe.

We hope that this book will be a source of inspiration and that the lessons of transformation we experienced and are now sharing with you will lift you up and enlighten you to make a difference in your life and your communities.

ATL Europe Board of Directors

Marie Diamond

Patrick Pype

Dr Cheryl Chapman

Dr Marion Bevington (Hon)

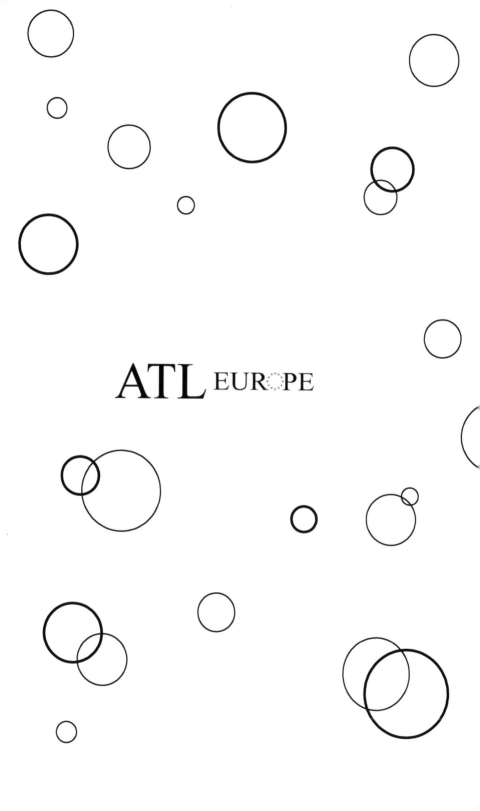

Chapter 1

SELF-LOVE:
WHAT IT IS AND WHAT IT ISN'T

Nikolina Balenović Knez

To start, I would like to tell you why I decided to write about this subject. I will share with you a little of my story. I don't remember much about my childhood. Those years are like a big black hole of nothingness. I do have memories of how I felt as a little me: being sad and lonely.

In my spiritual process of self-development, I found out that for people who had experienced a lot of traumas in their life, or been bullied or abused, it had felt so intense that they forgot their past in order to survive. That was my story too: I was bullied and verbally abused.

I had many problems in my life because I didn't love myself. I had problems in all my relationships, because I wanted my partners to love me. They did, but it was never enough for me, because I was needy for love – never enough. I had problems at work – I had some bosses who were bullies. I attracted them because my soul wanted to solve that wound. I was constantly criticising myself, belittling myself, being the worst enemy to myself, feeling that I was not worthy, that I was not good enough and that I was a mistake in this universe.

My childhood haunted me until I resolved my feelings. On my journey, many things helped me: therapists, healers, friends, spiritual education, and most of all my huge persistence. I wanted happiness to be my normal state of being, but instead sadness was. Even though I was cheerful and joyful with people, inside I was sad.

I did all that I could to change myself and eventually I succeeded in learning my lessons: 'To love myself and to see the world positively'.

Now, my most usual state is being OK with all who I am. I accept myself and I accept others and I love myself and my life. I have become the best parent to myself that I can possible be, the one that I always wanted my parents to be. In this process of my spiritual growth, I also educated myself to become an energy healer, feng shui adviser and life coach.

Now I help others in healing their wounds, to love themselves through spiritual mentoring, coaching and soul readings. I understood at one point in my life that all the badness happening to me was there to push me to heal myself and afterwards to heal others.

After many years of my inner search for self-love and through working with my dear clients on this topic, I would like to share with you what self-love is and what it isn't.

Self-love is:

- realising who you are, loving all that you are, accepting all your weaknesses and strengths, accepting all that is happening in your life – that will give you inner peace

- saying no when in your body you feel no

- saying yes – when you feel you have to do something and you do it even though you are scared

- listening and doing according to your intuition

- loving your body, which means listening to your body and doing what your body is saying to you every single day; realising that your body is your friend, not your enemy

- being guilt-free but aware and self-conscious and always being willing to go deeper

- doing every single day at least one thing that you love, and being brave enough to allow yourself to be truly who you are even though some people might judge you

Self-love is not:

- pleasing others in order for you to feel that you are a good person, nor is it thinking that others should do what you think they are supposed to be doing – those are expectations

- thinking that you are better than other people and behaving as though you are. No, there is no better. Yes, maybe you are more aware, yes maybe you are nicer, yes maybe you are smarter, yes maybe you are more respectful – but you are not better because of that, nor worse because of something else. You are a spark of the universe like everybody else. Putting yourself above others, that is not self-love, that is ego saying: "I am better than you." That is giving you false power

- judging others or yourself: instead, it is pure acceptance. Get rid of being right, instead be peaceful, get love into yourself and accept others

- a victim state, 'poor me' feeling. Self-love here would be to learn how to be strong and supportive to yourself instead of seeking energy and approval in other people

Find ways to love yourself, find a way to forgive yourself for not being 'perfect', forgive others – make this your number one priority. That is how I changed my life: I made it the most important task to embody in my life.

How can you start loving and accepting yourself?

That is a very important question. It took me years and years for that; now I mentor people how to do it.

Start with writing down all that is good about you and look and read that list with emotion every single day for at least six months until you embody it.

Listen to your feelings, respect them, don't judge them, don't say: "I am not supposed to feel that way." *No*, just simply accept what you feel. Listen to your body and do accordingly.

Don't let your mind rule your life; instead let your body and heart lead and then your mind can follow. If you do it in this order, everything will be in a beautiful flow.

Love yourself and accept others ♥

NIKOLINA BALENOVIĆ KNEZ

Nikolina Balenović Knez is a spiritual teacher, intuitive soul coach and mentor, soul reader, healer, ThetaHealing® practitioner and feng shui consultant. She has been on several courses on intuition, channelling and spirituality led by Sonia Choquette and others. She is from Croatia and has a Bachelor of Economics degree.

Nikolina's greatest passion is to work with people on their personal transformation of self-love through a spiritual approach and to empower others to be the authentically best version of themselves. She is a talented and powerful intuitive counsellor. She sees deeply and accurately into people's lives and can provide powerful guidance and insights. She is gifted at giving her clients energy and support to change their lives in the most profound ways.

Nikolina is a member of ATL Europe.

www.beautifulspirit.net/
www.sretanzivot.hr/
www.facebook.com/beautifulspirit.net/
www.facebook.com/Sretan-zivot-1435571473335535/
www.youtube.com/channel/UC59TYtIWa43JsfLusdHJCaQ
www.instagram.com/nikolinabalenovicknez/

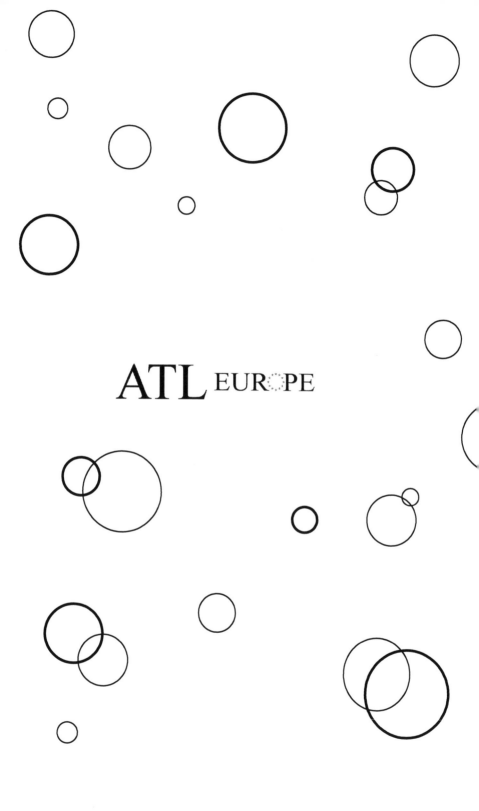

Chapter 2

VITALITY BEGINS WITH YOU

Dr Gill Barham

On 1 November 2012, I was asked this question by a petite, white-haired nurse who looked over her glasses at me as she held my appalling test results: "Gill, have you had any thoughts of harming yourself?" To say I was shocked is an understatement. I thought that at 51 years old I was coping with my busy life – supporting my husband through setting up his own business after redundancy; supporting my children through exams (and more exams), their moving to university, their friendship issues and social pressures; and supporting my son through his recent life-threatening illness. I was in the depths of managing my father's dementia and the stressful relationships with both of my brothers, plus coping with a job outside my natural field, and more significantly 'managing-up' an ineffective boss. So, you see, I was practically Superwoman!

Except I was fat, sick and unhappy. My spiral into depression and illness was so gradual that neither I, nor those close to me, had really recognised what was happening. That is, until I began the road to recovery when the real wife, mum, friend, colleague, singer, funny and unique woman re-emerged. The path to joy, vitality and fulfilment has been at times challenging, but I am so grateful for the lessons, and the people along the way who have been, and continue to be, my salvation and helped me avoid the outcome that my mother – who died at just 56 years old – suffered.

You see, this lightbulb question made me re-evaluate my life and, in that moment, I had to decide whether I was going to set a good example to my loved ones or be a horrible warning, just like that of my dear Mum who at 51 had almost the exact same symptoms, but was also suicidal.

So where do I begin?

As a nurse, I was aware of the side effects of medication and refused the offer of antidepressants but did accept some counselling. The real kick-start back to health was through my concentrated efforts to look after my diet, to find time for myself, and to move more every day. I *knew* what I was supposed to do as I had access to advice from friends and colleagues and many conventional, alternate, and complementary health professionals including Dr Google. Perhaps like you though, I realised that *knowing* is not *doing*. So I began to change things gradually: I found people to help me; I began exercising by dancing to videos, to read and research, and to love and accept myself. I started to change the way I ate and added in high-quality vitamins and supplements. As I began to feel better and recognise that I had been consoling myself with food, my body and my spirit changed.

Food as medicine

You may have heard the expression: 'We are what we eat'. Even Hippocrates, the Greek physician, knew his onions: "Let food be thy medicine, let medicine be thy food." I wholeheartedly believe now that we need to adopt a return to 'clean eating': cooking foods from fresh and sourcing foods that have high levels of nutrients, vitamins and essential minerals. In other words, what our grandparents called 'food' and we now call 'organic food'. I would like to encourage you to buy food that is in season from your local markets and cook from fresh, sitting at a table to enjoy eating with your loved ones as frequently as possible.

I know, I know… I hear you say: "But I'm so busy, my kids and partner won't eat green veg, I can't afford to shop for organic foods, I buy healthy salads and ready meals from my supermarket and deli, they must be OK? I eat out too often, I am always travelling, I don't know where to start!"

You may say: "It all sounds like hard work, sounds expensive, sounds too time-consuming, sounds too complicated, sounds too scary, sounds too stressful." But ask anyone with a chronic illness, such as cancer or heart disease: "What is your experience of illness?" they will agree: it is hard work, it's expensive, time-consuming, complicated, scary, and stressful.

It's all about stacking the cards in your favour

Here are a few tips to achieving elite health and vitality. You could start by cutting the CRAP:

- C – caffeine: a stimulant that disrupts messages to your brain, masking tiredness, and therefore raising stress levels in the body.

- R – refined sugars: not just the sugar in your tea or coffee but also foods that convert to sugar quickly in the bloodstream (bread, pasta, rice, white potatoes and associated products like rice cakes).

- A – alcohol: high in sugar, influences your acid/alkaline balance.

- P – processed foods: containing additives and preservatives, 'endocrine disruptors', 'bad fats' that produce inflammation in the body, and fried or barbecued foods, because of associated toxins.

The extent to how careful you are with your food will determine your longevity, but I feel I need to reiterate here that it is not the *whole* story, otherwise the clean eaters and vegans of the world would all avoid illness and that simply isn't the case. However, it is true that those with the healthiest diets have less incidence of disease, but we must also look more holistically and examine the effect that your habits, relationships, emotions and past traumas have on your physical and mental wellbeing too.

So, I have a few questions for you to ponder on:

- Are you doing something that you are passionate about?
- Are those with whom you spend time lifting you up or bringing you down?
- Are you contributing to your community and family?
- What is your work-life balance like?
- How do you feel emotionally?
- Are you physically as fit as you would like?
- Are you financially secure?
- Are you setting a good example?

As I continue to grow, to age gracefully, to feel happier and healthier, and to connect on a deeper level to what and who is important, I invite you to join me on this transformational journey.

DR GILL BARHAM

Dr Gill Barham is a broadcast presenter, speaker, author and advocate for mental and social health prevention, as well as being a Pilates teacher and functional nutritionist. She has transformed the health and outlook of her many readers, clients and followers.

Her book, *The Heart of a Woman: How to look after the heart you give to the world*, is a guide to healthy longevity for women, but is a must-read for every man with a special female in their life. Gill has also created, collaborated on, or contributed to four other books to date.

Gill lives in rural Northamptonshire with her husband Peter. She is a singer and musician, and loves to walk, read, cook, ski, fish for salmon as well as spending time on the family's narrow boat. She has three talented and loving grown-up children, Ellie, Matthew and Lydia, whom she describes as her best achievements to date.

www.drgillbarham.com
twitter.com/GillBarham
www.facebook.com/DrGillBarham
www.linkedin.com/in/drgillbarham
www.instagram.com/richwomanretreats

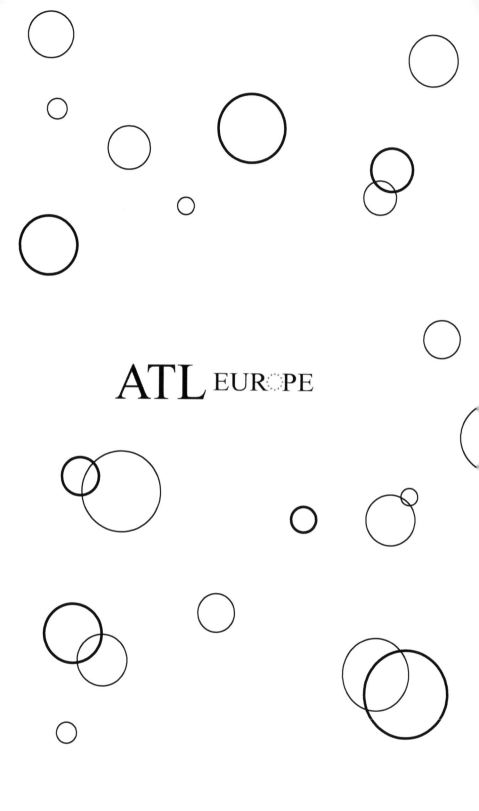

Chapter 3

OUR TIME IS NOW

Bea Benkova

It's October 2007, the first day of our honeymoon. I'm sitting on the rooftop terrace of the George V hotel in Athens with my husband Jan, overlooking the Acropolis, immersed in the soft warmth of the sunset. I feel this is the start of something much bigger than just the two of us. I take a deep sigh. It's been a year of life transformative changes. A year since I began to shed things that no longer served me, including my 'dream career' in investment banking. I have been on a year-long journey enquiring deep into myself to find the answers to these three questions: "*Who am I? Why am I here? Where am I going?*"

The answers to the questions are emerging. Now I am clear that I am the possibility of transformation of humanity and I am here to fulfil on this purpose. It sounds overwhelming, yet so exciting. But then my energy drops. I turn to Jan and ask him: "How can I ground this in reality? What should I do next?"

Jan asks me: "What have you discovered speaking to futurists, entrepreneurs and business leaders about what is coming to us from the future and what is required of humankind?"

"There is so much I have learned from them," I explain. "There seems to be an underlying message of the re-emergence of the divine feminine on our planet, and that women are the catalysts of this global shift." Jan looks puzzled yet fascinated. I turn my head back to look at the sunset and far ahead. "Yes, women," I repeat. It suddenly becomes clear to me. Over the past 50 years women have been increasingly stepping up into positions of power and authority. Presidents, prime ministers, chief executives: women are leading in all sectors. As women we are gaining power. I can see, however, that in many instances by the time we get there we are no longer being women. I am seeing that being a woman does not equal being feminine. We are being like men.

What are we losing? What are we depriving the world of? The world is suffering without our divine feminine essence. As I look into the sunset, I feel myself melting into the changing colours, becoming one with the cycles of the universe. Endings and beginnings. And then I feel it. The divine feminine, the anima mundi. The soul of the universe.

And in that moment a vision appears before my eyes. I see a wide-open space filled with women. Each woman glowing, empowered, fulfilled, living her purpose. Moving together in unison with the waves, pushing the boundaries of the ocean, breaking new ground. Leading the way for humanity to higher evolution. It is so magical and potent. It takes my breath away. This is the Constellation of Extraordinary Women. This is why I am here. To create such a strong and protective space for women, so that they can fully integrate their feminine and masculine energies, align themselves with their purpose and ground their visions, together.

Rise of the divine feminine

A Cherokee prophecy reveals that there will be a time when the bird of humanity realises it has been flying with just one wing. The male wing getting almost violent trying to keep humanity afloat. But when the other wing, the female wing, expresses itself, the male wing can relax and the bird of humanity will soar. The 'divine feminine' is the wise universal goddess that has existed since the beginning of time, rooted in the earth, in absolute respect for Gaia and her interconnected systems that sustain beauty and life.

At this critical time for humanity, we are facing global challenges that no other generation has faced before. The survival of the world depends on the divine feminine. We must all, men and women, embrace the divine feminine and lead through intuition, collaboration and synergies, bringing forth a sustainable, resilient and inclusive human presence on the planet.

Aligned power of extraordinary women

In 2009, the Dalai Lama astounded the world by declaring that "The world will be saved by the western woman." I had a deep knowing that he was not referring to one particular woman, but to a community of women acting as one. This community is a constellation of extraordinary women, calibrated with each other, collectively acting as a unified force to transform humanity.

If ever there comes a time when the women of the world come together purely and simply for the benefit of mankind, it will be a force such as the world has never known.

Matthew Arnold, philosopher and poet

In 2012, I created the Global Institute for Extraordinary Women (GIFEW). Inside the constellation, every woman finds her unique place, which is aligned with her talent, passion and purpose, a place that nurtures her to create her vision for her life that expresses her legacy. This is her rightful place in the sky and society. From that unique place, she creates synergies with other women in the constellation to create the aligned power. All sectors of our society are interconnected and are a critical part of our societal ecosystem. When we align our divine feminine power together, we can heal the world and transform our societies. As my friend Jazz Rasool says: "No one remembers a star in the sky. But everyone remembers a constellation."

Our time is now

I can see as clear as daylight that the hour is coming when women will lead humanity to a higher evolution.

Hazrat Inayat Khan

The time has come for a quantum leap in evolutionary consciousness. We are all responsible for the condition of our world as it is, and its future. The future of humanity is not something outside you. It is you. Transformation begins with you. Do not live by the constraints of your past, your culture and your fears. Express yourself, fulfil your destiny.

Our time is now. #togetherwerise

BEA BENKOVA

Bea Benkova is a European transformational leader and founder of the Global Institute for Extraordinary Women (GIFEW).

Originally from Slovakia, Bea was raised believing that she can make a difference in the world. Since leaving the banking world in 2007, Bea has inspired, empowered and guided prominent women around the world – including leading executives, entrepreneurs, politicians and artists – to discover and express their unique purpose, femininity, and leadership.

In 2012 Bea founded the GIFEW to expand on her vision of the transformation of humanity through the aligned power of extraordinary women. GIFEW is dedicated to the holistic, collaborative and transformational education of women around world and over the first years of its existence has made a difference to hundreds of women across five continents.

Bea and her husband, Jan Polak, currently share their time between their two residences in London, England and Bratislava, Slovakia.

www.gifew.org

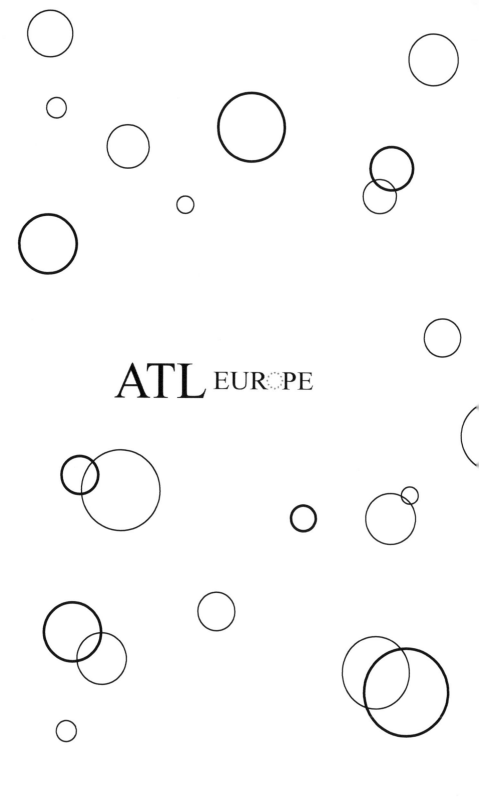

Chapter 4

OOZING JUICY JOY

Dr Marion Bevington (Hon)

I believe that as humans part of our role, or maybe even our destiny, is to discover ways to experience happiness. This is certainly true for me. As a kid, whenever I was asked that proverbial question: "What do you want to be when you grow up?" my reply was always: "Happy!" After my 54 journeys around the sun, I have realised that the experience of happiness can be temporary, *but* I now know it's possible to celebrate all of life − the ups and the downs − and remain joyful. So how to live in this state of joy?

While it's true that happiness is all in your mind, it is also true that when the body is uncomfortable or in pain or feeling out of sorts in any way, this will always influence the mind and will affect the levels of happiness you experience. For over 40 years I was outwardly successful, but also inwardly tortured. A successful student of mathematics and computer science, I went on to become a computer programmer, eventually managing technical teams and projects with multimillion-pound budgets. I found it easy to fulfil the academic and corporate demands placed on me and so to all intents and purposes was deemed 'successful' by society.

My pockets were full but my heart felt empty, disconnected and unloved. I spent over 20 years working to fund my otherwise vagabond lifestyle. Travelling became my salvation and I have visited and lived in some amazing places: from London to Lima, from Amazonia to Zanzibar, from Toxteth to Timbuktu. It became clear to me that I was running from the emptiness I felt, that inward torture, but since it was inside I could never escape it. A traumatic childhood had left a residue of old fear and tension patterns in my body and mind – hidden from me until I got sick and began my own journey back to wholeness, to that juicy joy I'd been oozing as a baby before life and conditioning took hold.

How do you ooze juicy joy so much so that it becomes infectious, so it influences and affects others? To show them how to feel a sense of contentment, connection and love?

To begin this journey to juicy joy, let's start with a fundamental part of your body: your connective tissue, also known as fascia. What I learned about biology at school was it's thought of as 'useless white stuff' that was just the packaging material, the cling film for the 'more important' muscles and organs. But now fascia has grabbed the attention of scientists, teachers and therapists all over the world: this tissue is now known to be so important it has whole universities and academies devoted to studying and understanding it.

Fascia is the organ of wholeness. It is everywhere. It is the matrix of your body, weaving its way through the whole of you. It's like a huge strong, flexible web, full of pockets into which everything else in the body is embedded, and through which everything else communicates and functions.

Everything in your body needs the fascia to be juicy to express and receive information because it is the foundation of all communication needed to function. When it's juicy, it's flexible, resilient, it will twist and bend, it remains springy and elastic. In its healthy state fascia is relaxed. It can stretch without restriction. When any force is applied to juicy fascia, it is distributed through the entire network of the body evenly. If you fall on your hip, your juicy fascia will transmit the force throughout the body, making injury less likely. Babies have loads of juicy fascia and this makes them seem almost rubbery.

When fascia isn't juicy it can get brittle and is prone to tearing and damage. When experiencing physical, emotional, mental or in fact any kind of trauma, scarring or inflammation, fascia begins to tighten up and become matted, rigid, knotted and lumpy, which then results in it drying out as the juiciness cannot flow. Trauma ranging from surgery or car accidents to habitual poor posture and repetitive stress all accumulate as they affect the body, preventing your ability to function comfortably and easily.

Restricted fascia may result in pain, headaches, restricted movement, weakened muscles, decreased circulation of fluids leading to high blood pressure, lower immune function and hormone imbalance, affecting your ability to withstand stress and perform your routine daily activities.

Unbalanced fascia has a domino effect and creates compensatory patterns that can affect all the systems of your body, including your nervous system, your cardiovascular system and your immune system. Learning how to keep your fascia juicy so it's more elastic and can communicate more effectively means all systems of your body can work together in a more integrated way.

Oozing juicy joy – so that's the theory, now let's begin the five-step journey.

To perceive the world around you, you use the five senses, right? To connect deeply to the whole of you and the world takes eight senses. (Dr. Dan Seigel from the book *Mindsight - The New Science of Personal Transformation.*)

Step 1. Safety (five senses), using your sight, hearing, smell, taste and touch, notice where you are and what's around you. If you are not feeling safe, then move to a place that feels safe.

Step 2. Scan your inner state (activate sixth sense), connect to your body sensations, find a place of inner strength and comfort.

Step 3. Sense your inner being (sixth sense) take a few slow breaths and allow the body to relax.

Step 4. Stir (seventh sense) notice any mental stirrings and activities such as feelings, thoughts, and memories. Remain compassionate and allow what surfaces without judgment.

Step 5. Spiritual connection (eighth sense) – our relationships to other people and to the planet. (This is automatic and happens as a result of activating the other seven senses.)

Remember, everything is connected inside and out; spending time on each step takes you closer to your own juicy joy.

DR MARION BEVINGTON (Hon)

"I used to program computers – now I de-program people."

A diagnosis of two 'incurable autoimmune conditions' woke Marion to decide her health and wellness must take priority. By accessing the super-intelligent body she has now reversed almost all the symptoms without medication or surgery.

Marion now works in multiple businesses and has won awards for coaching, teaching and as an author.

Founder of Corporate Yoga London and Stage Fright Away, she helps people to enjoy presenting, performing and speaking up as their authentic selves. Marion is a co-creator of the Find Your WHY! Foundation, which helps people to Find their WHY! and become frickin' awesome.

In 2017 Marion was awarded an honorary doctorate for global leadership and peace initiatives.

www.marionbevington.com/
www.facebook.com/marion.bevington
www.linkedin.com/in/marionbevington/
plus.google.com/u/0/+MarionBevington
www.instagram.com/drmarionbevington/

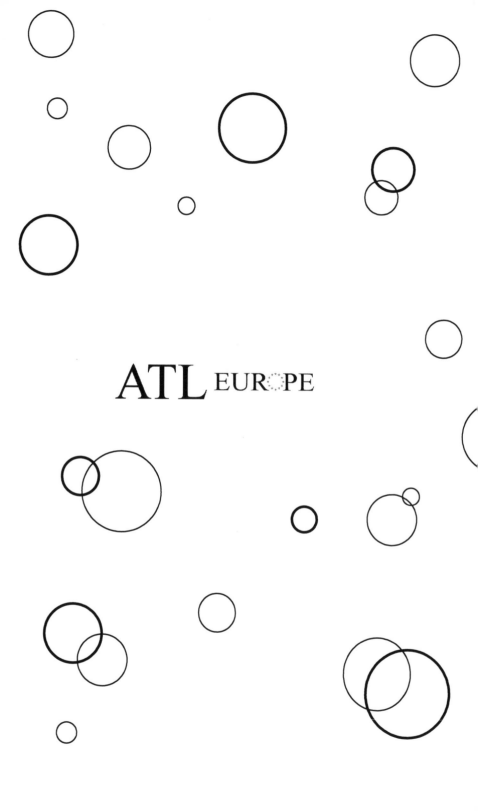

Chapter 5

HAVE YOU EVER BEEN AT A CROSSROADS IN YOUR LIFE?

Dr Cheryl Chapman

It's August 2011 and looking around I can see the slatted panels that are covering the walls of the 6 x 2-metre box that I'm sitting in. Despite the shipping container 'office' standing in a warm, stuffy warehouse, there is a cold chill in the air. He looks at me with his dark, piercing eyes; in these moments he really does look like Dracula. "So, Cheryl, when I called you last week from China, it took you 23 minutes to reply:

u-n-a-c-c-e-p-t-a-b-l-e."

Have you ever had a time in your life when you felt judged? As though you weren't good enough? I can't wait to get home and see my two best friends: Gordon, with his white cap and broad shoulders, who helps me chill; and Stella, my European friend, who makes me feel a bit feisty.

As I unscrew the white cap on the Gordon's gin bottle and pull back the ring on the can of Stella lager, I feel at home. Have you ever tried to distract from your life? I'd like to tell you that that was the only night I spent with my 'friends', however, if there was a 'y' in the day, Stella, Gordon and I were, well, having a ***ménage à trois.***

I stumbled into personal development, originally through Bob Proctor who introduced me to new words such as 'paradigms' and 'positive thinking'. Don't get me wrong – I had a library of books on the subject, books that I'd never read. I went to see Bob in London and that's where another speaker called Andy Harrington came on to the stage and asked: "If you were to die tomorrow, who would mourn your loss?" With 43 friends on Facebook, I guessed that wasn't going to be a lot. And then he said: "If that number is small, you have led an insignificant life." In that moment, I realised that something needed to change, I was a 48-year-old alcoholic who hated her life. Truth be known, I may as well have been in a box, yes, a coffin.

It's said that when the student is ready the master will appear. For me, that is when I met Dr Marion Bevington. She's like the female version of Indiana Jones: she's travelled the world looking for treasure and ancient wisdom, and she could see that I had some blocks. Using kinesiology, she was able to ask my body to find what was holding me back. It turned out that a conversation with my mum when I was five had led to me being 'careful' about what others might say and keeping secrets. I began to think 'out of the box' and became fascinated about how such childhood experiences could affect adults. I realised that a trauma in childhood doesn't always have to be horrific, I mean dropping an ice cream when you're five years old is a trauma, right?

I studied neurolinguistic programming (NLP), life coaching and rapid transformational therapy with the incredible Marisa Peer, and I read and listened to anything and everything about the subject. And I started to take action in my own life too. I learned the art of public speaking and travelled the world, making a difference in thousands of people's lives.

In June 2015, I gave up drinking because I realised I loved my life and so no longer needed distraction. With this newfound clarity and drive, I realised I was living my purpose: I'd found my 'why'!

In 2016 Marion and I created The Find Your WHY! Foundation because we have realised that there are just three areas that you need to master to be able to find your 'why'. These are *'awareness'*, *'intention'* and *'manifest'* (also known as move into action).

Your 'why' comes in two guises:

- Why are you where you are right now in your life? What is good and what is no longer serving you? Unless you know this, it's like getting into a car with a satellite navigation system and not knowing what co-ordinates to put in for the starting point.

- What's your purpose? Here's something you can do right now to get you closer to finding the answer. Revisit your past to find out what you loved doing as a child or teenager. Go back to four scenes in your mind and make a note of all the times you felt happy: what are you doing, who are you with and how are you feeling?

Now look for the links: this simple exercise starts to give you the answer to your why. Looking back, my scenes included a debate in school about women's place in the world, making others smile for the camera, standing up for my friends, and being told that I could be the next prime minister of the UK. I realised that my why was always about standing up and speaking out, helping others to be happy too. Now the only box I use is a soapbox, to share messages of hope and help.

You see, however small or large trauma is, it's the reason why many of my clients feel afraid of taking action, feel they're not good enough and are afraid of failure, success, judgment and rejection. My 'why' is to guide others to find their 'why', so they can become the person they were born to be.

I'm now on a global mission to guide 10 million disheartened souls to go from 'Why me?' to 'Why not me?'

So, here's the thing, when you find your 'why', you can live a life that inspires you, fires you up, makes you smile – a life where you are happy and where you know you are making a difference.

If you don't know your 'why', well, you might end up living someone else's.

DR CHERYL CHAPMAN

Dr Cheryl Chapman is an multi-award-winning international speaker, author, mentor and director of ATL (Europe).

She is co-author of the award-winning book, *Find Your Why: become Frickin' Awesome* and the co-creator of the Find Your WHY Foundation, where she teaches the 'A.I.M to Find Your WHY Program' which was developed with fellow ATL director, Dr Marion Bevington. The program helps others gain clarity about their 'why', so that they can live a life of passion, purpose and fulfilment.

Cheryl shares her message internationally and her clients are based worldwide, including in Australia, Malaysia, Thailand, Singapore, South Africa, Canada, UAE, Europe and UK. Cheryl is a trained NLP master practitioner and a rapid transformational therapist. As an award-winning speaker and trainer, she has trained thousands of people to share their messages to others. She was awarded an honorary doctorate in 2017 for leadership and global peace work.

www.findyourwhyfoundation.com/
www.facebook.com/FindYourWhyToBecomeFrickinAwesome/
www.linkedin.com/in/cherylchapman29/
www.instagram.com/drcheryl.chapman29
twitter.com/cherylchapman_

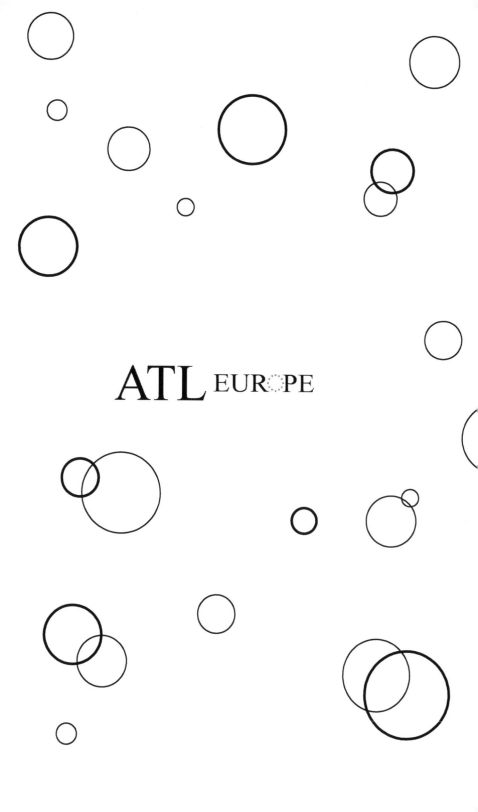

Chapter 6

LESSONS FROM THE LOBSTER POT: LETTING GO OF SUCCESS IN ORDER TO SUCCEED

Miranda Christopher

At what point does the lobster being slowly boiled alive realise its fate? For me it was when, in 2014, I awoke with the most intense pain in my head – unable to move, to speak clearly or retain my balance. It was on that day that I finally understood that life had turned up the stress level just a little too much. Looking back, the warning signs were there, with the odd 'nothing to be too concerned about' illnesses, the constant fatigue and the perpetual sense of battling on. How often are we so stoic about these things?

I recall being asked at a job interview, when my children were small, what I intended to do with regard to my childcare while I was at work. Keeping a straight face, I reassured my two male interviewers that the children were kept safe and well in a cupboard under the stairs with plenty of bread and water. I was amused by their unsure responses! Humour aside, in reality, I was juggling childcare arrangements between family members and a day care facility, long hours commuting and running the household – all at the same time as doing advanced study to climb up the corporate ladder. This was pretty much the pattern set for the rest of my career and I know that this is the standard for most women wanting to have a career alongside raising a family. And yes, some men experience it too.

It was a straightforward decision to become an independent consultant. I was doing similar work while being paid significantly more, with the added bonus of being able to spend more time with my children in the holidays. I can't pretend it was easy, because it was far from that: I was constantly walking a fine line, often being knocked sideways, berating myself for not being good enough as a mother.

The downside of my illness was that I was unable to work. Even when the physical symptoms subsided, it seemed that I had been robbed of my confidence. For the first time in my adult life, I was totally financially dependent on another human being and that wasn't easy. I am so grateful for my ever-patient husband. To say I felt lost, unsure of who I really was and unable to paint a positive picture for my future was an understatement. However, the gift in the illness was time.

Time to ponder, to reflect, to learn and to ask why. Initially I was in a pity party for one and my sole question was: "Why me?" I knew I was stuck, I knew I had to do something about my situation, but I just didn't know how. I had shifted from being a total fun-loving socialising diva to being an anti-people hermit.

I did what we all do at those times: I turned to my trusty companion Google®. **The answers revealed by this font of all knowledge suggested that I attend a personal development event for women.** In all honesty I almost didn't walk through the door, my confidence was so low. But I am so glad I did.

My questions about why turned to my observations of the women in the group. Why did one woman seem to have no issue with generating new business, yet others did? Why did women leaving the corporate world struggle to move forward with their business?

Why did a highly successful career woman struggle with depression when she became her own boss? My questions led a two-year research project – and the findings were intriguing. What would you do with all this information? Of course, you'd test it. And that's what I did.

Our current business model has been around for several hundred years. It was designed by a few for their own benefit. They provided structures and ways of working that organised the masses, with the balance of power being of a certain demographic: male, white and affluent. It's a world that has struggled to adapt to the needs of an ambitious female workforce.

What my findings highlight is that it is time for a paradigm shift in business. A transformation like no other, one that would take the collaboration of many – and the journey starts inside each and every one of us. We must let go of what no longer serves us and rise as a beacon of hope for all humanity. Change the way we do business and we literally change the world.

Consider this, dear reader: buried inside is the pure authentic you. Over the years you have been conditioned. Let me show you how. Think now of the word **success**, on the surface an innocuous seven-letter word. If you take the time to ponder it, to observe the thoughts it evokes, to notice the sensations you experience, the images it conjures, I am sure that you, like me, will come to realise that maybe you have striven in life for things that were conditioned by our parents, by our religion, from within our education system and our careers. To get a good job, to have a nice home and maybe to chase the money.

That gift of time allowed me to recognise that I personally had to let go of everything that was tied to that word. Success no longer meant a nine-to-five job, which in reality is a seven-to-seven. It no longer meant playing mind games in business. It no longer meant a group of unknown people determining my worth, my value. It no longer meant a working environment that doesn't understand the changes a woman's body goes through in her lifetime. I had to get out of that lobster pot! I had to let go of success in order to succeed. Now, what do you need to let go of?

MIRANDA CHRISTOPHER

Miranda Christopher is the founder of The Minerva Directory, a platform for female business owners to learn, share and grow stronger together. She is also a teacher and mentor for women moving from corporate employment to being their own bosses, and a coach for people seeking to be leaders in their lives, in their businesses and in their careers.

Miranda spent more than 25 years in corporate organisations leading large-scale transformational activity, working with leading global brands to implement more effective ways of working in order to increase profitability. Today, Miranda's passion is to help women step up in business, to create solid foundations for growth, to find their voices and make their presence known. She helps them live and do business by their rules, rather than by the expected norms, helping women to change the way we do business.

"It's my business to finish the unfinished business of the 21st century: female empowerment for gender equality."

www.minerva.directory
miranda@minerva.directory
https://twitter.com/fembizplatform
https://www.facebook.com/theminervadirectory/
https://www.instagram.com/minervadirectory
www.mirandachristopher.co.uk

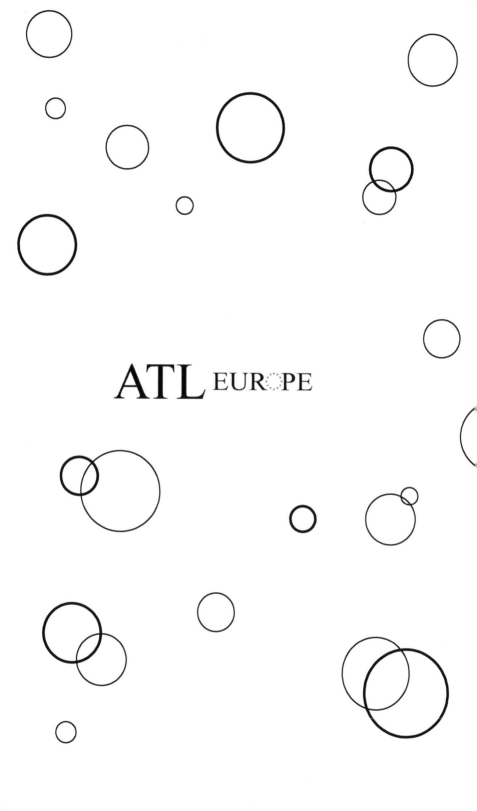

Chapter 7

DARE TO BE NAKED

Sandra Deakin

I believe when you have the courage to be nakedly honest in life you will be supported by the universe with more vitality, enriching relationships and an inner radiating beauty. Because behind all your masks is your purest essence waiting to shine. Some call it 'love', others 'truth' or 'grace'. You all have your unique perfume.

I have discovered that everything outside yourself is just a projection of who you are at that moment. So, stop pointing your finger and start looking inside. The more you strip down the stories in your mind, the more the outside world will reflect our inner spark.

It took me years to realise this and to live it. As a television and radio personality, I was quite good at hiding behind several masks. I felt much safer with my make-up and designer clothes. Other masks would be my enthusiastic smile or the sweet girl always trying to 'please' everybody.

Everything was always so wonderful through my eyes and I did not realise that I was constantly denying my own pain and darkness.

Until my body showed me the naked truth by being in 'dis-ease'.

I fell into a deep dark hole, and that was scary for someone who had always been 'little sunshine'. That was the moment I discovered I had never been 'enough'. All my life I had been looking for approval. Because of that I had completely neglected my inside world.

For years my body, my inner little girl and the woman in me had been starving and crying for help. I had refused to listen. On the contrary, when they were shouting I narcotised myself by working even harder.

As an interviewer, I specialised in seeking the true essence of my guests. Today, I realise I had been looking only for my own inner light in the eyes of others.

Some of them had spoken about 'the dark night of the soul'. Being 'little miss bright spot', I had never allowed any darkness in my life.

Until the moment when all I thought I was falling into smithereens. My work did not give me that fulfilment any longer, my relationship with my husband had a temporary breakdown and my body no longer functioned the way I wanted it to. I guess that was my dark night of the soul. Luckily, the universe was sending me 'by coincidence' some beautiful souls who had already been there. One by one they guided me to a bright spot in my darkness.

The first thing I learned was how to live in my body. I had neglected this beautiful temple of mine for years. I decided to start listening to my physical being and went into deep silence. I discovered that the body is like a sponge; it sucks up every emotion ever denied and every conscious or subconscious thought pattern.

It took me years to clean up my inner garden: the hidden tears and fears, the suppressed anger. All came out just like loud little children wanting to be heard and embraced. I knew that if I ever wanted to get on my feet again and enjoy life I had to get nakedly honest with myself.

That needed a lot of courage, because behind the facade of the cool happy media woman was a very scared little girl begging for love and affection. So, I met my inner little girl, whom I had denied for years. And oh dear, did she give me a hard time! She was furious because of this neglect. After the waves of fear and sadness, the anger came out.

And I learned to welcome and embrace it all without judgment, no story attached, just love and acceptance.

After discovering the little girl, the hungry woman appeared. I had also blocked her out completely. Although I looked very feminine and sensual on the outside, my so-called 'career' life had turned me into a living masculine power woman in a well-shaped feminine body. How contradictory could that be.

Another bright spot turned up in my darkness and taught me how to reclaim my 'sexual energy'. I became a radiant queen simply by living inside my womb. This gave me a feeling of coming home. The moment my heart became rooted in mother earth it felt safe enough to open wider. It was amazing how, suddenly, I gained more vitality and sexual power. This healed my body and I learned how to use my orgasmic energy to create and manifest.

Today the queen inside me can sit on her throne and radiate her love. She is enough as she is and she enjoys life the fullest. She gets equality and respect from her husband. Each day we look upon each other as new.

To be able to live this more enlightened way, I have to be nakedly honest with myself and fully present in my body. And when I get tempted to start living in lies again the body responds immediately.

I'd love to share one of my daily tools with you on how to start living in your body and revitalise it. The secret is a simple inviting touch.

Just close your eyes. Gently touch your heart. Smile through your hands. Breathe into your heart a soft red light. Sigh out all the darkness hidden inside you. Let all your thoughts drop like stones into the darkness of your pelvic bowl. Make soft circular movements from left to right around your belly button. 'Invite' the body in a smiling way to open and release all that is no longer serving you.

When emotions come, embrace them with all your love. Stop the story in your mind. Just feel the sensation in your body in all honesty.

I promise you when you make this a daily ritual your body will become your best navigator in life.

Good luck!

SANDRA DEAKIN

Offering people bright spots in their life has always been a passion for Sandra Deakin. From the age of 14, she was a radio presenter.

Sandra has created several television shows in Belgium. She is known to be a pioneer in guiding her audience to a more enlightened way of living. Today, she presents on the Belgian Radio 2 channel, reaching more than 1 million listeners. Her global online telesummit: *Celebrate Her*, in which she interviewed inspiring women on how to live a more enlightened life, reached 300,000 viewers.

As a writer, Sandra has created two lifestyle guides in which she selects juicy hotspots in her city, Antwerp.

She has interviewed more than 100 global transformers for several lifestyle magazines. Sandra guides people worldwide on how to live a more enlightened life in a happy body. She is currently writing her book on how to find bright spots in your life and has her own online channel, *Bright Spots*.

www.brightspots.be
www.brightspots.eu
sandra.deakin1@gmail.com
www.facebook.com/sandra.deakin.75
www.instagram.com/brightspotsbysandra

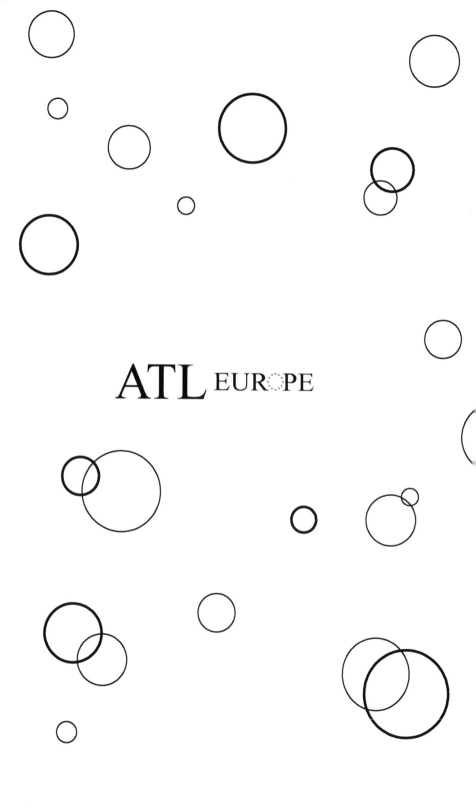

Chapter 8

THE BLOSSOMING OF A YOUNG WOMAN WITH A PASSION

Enya Demeyer

Yes, at just 14, I am an advocate for women's rights. Am I too young? I believe not. If I am old enough to be catcalled, then I am old enough to have an opinion about being catcalled. So, without further ado, let us begin.

Like most young women, I go to school. And there, I hear many stupid things being said that are simply the result of ignorance. "You run like a girl!" Well, thank you very much. I do run like a girl. Because, believe it or not, I am a girl. "Go to the kitchen and make me a sandwich." Well, I do love sandwiches, but how about you use your two hands and make me one too (extra mayonnaise, please). What's worse is that when I decide to tell teachers about it, they reply with the same, outdated saying: "Boys will be boys." Ah yes, I've heard those words a fair amount in only a decade and four years of being alive, and I'm sick of it. But that's only the beginning.

When I turned 13, things escalated. So, let me paint you a picture. It's 2017, a beautiful summer day. I am walking to the beach in a floral dress, completely minding my own business. At this point, I'm living in Monaco and naturally, many fancy cars that I couldn't care less about pass by. Suddenly, an orange Lamborghini slows down to a walking pace right beside me. Getting more and more paranoid, I start speeding up. Lo and behold, it follows me. The man inside it rolls down his window and says: "Hey pretty girl, come into my car, I can show you a good time." This man is about 30. Ew. This, ladies and gentlemen, is an example of catcalling. And what is more, he is catcalling a minor. Naturally, I don't like this at all. Instinctively I raise my hand and show them a rather rude finger. He drives away.

Sadly, this wasn't the last time it happened to me.

Many people have told me that in my future career, I will not be paid the same amount as my fellow male colleagues. Excuse me? When I first heard this, I couldn't believe it. But with further research, I realised that there is a 20% gender pay gap. Great, so not only will men be asking me to make them sandwiches all the time, harassing me when I walk down a street, but now I won't even be paid the same as them simply because my anatomy is different? Weeks of frustration and injustice pass and nothing happened. Well, surely anger will solve this problem, right? No. It will not. I realised that a solution to this thousand-year-old problem won't just appear out of the blue, I would have to work for it.

I welcome you to an article about the blossoming of a young feminist.

At this moment in time, I am only at the beginning of my transformational experience. I write speeches about my passion for women's rights, educate people on the topic and get together with other people who share my thoughts and hope to learn from them. But there is so much more I would like to accomplish. I want to march for women's rights one day. I want to become a UN representative for women's rights. I want to go down in history as a powerful woman who fought for her rights. This may sound extremely ambitious, but I believe in myself.

The lesson of this chapter is to find your passion, and then live out your transformational process. In the beginning, you may seem lost. How can I ever move forward? It's simple. Set goals for yourself and work hard to achieve them. Opportunities won't simply be handed to you: hand them to yourself. Don't doubt what you're capable of, instead be excited for what's to come. A passion is something that sets out the path of your life, something that you know you will work hard for. I'm passionate about women's rights. Alongside many powerful women and men, we will make a change. What are you passionate about? Once you find it, make a change with it.

Now you may be thinking, why should I take advice from a 14 year old? That's a very good question, indeed. I am, after all, a teenager who has been on this planet only for a short amount of time. But I am the future of this planet. And whether people like it or not, the youth is making an effort to do its part in creating a better place. "The millennials are lazy." Well, you can say that, but in my opinion, marching the streets for our rights isn't what I call lazy.

After all I have said, I'm not asking you blossom into a feminist, burn your bra and passionately protest for equality. I ask of you to consider, reflect on and process what I have said. I have faith that I will be paid the same amount as my fellow male colleagues. I have hope that when I walk the streets I will be treated with respect, not a woman you can take advantage of. I am confident that I will help make all these things happen. Because I am not a weak, unstable woman. I am powerful, and I can make a change. Find your passion, and truly be passionate about it. Find your passion, and make a change.

ENYA DEMEYER

Enya Demeyer was born in Santa Barbara, California, USA in 2003 and now lives in London, UK. She is the co-founder of ATL Junior and daughter of Marie Diamond, founder of ATL Europe.

Her passions are public speaking, musical theatre, singing and women's rights. She speaks four languages and has lived in more than eight countries.

Enya participated in the model United Nations and raised money for education in Bolivia. She studies in the London Academy of Music and Dramatic Art and participates successfully in international speaking contests.

Enya is also a certified diamond dowser, meditates daily and practices the law of attraction and feng shui.

www.instagram.com/enyaeny.a
www.enyademeyer.com

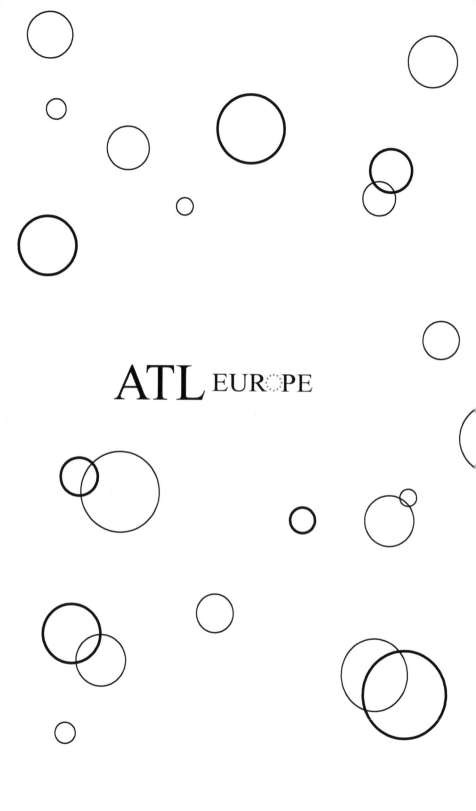

Chapter 9

FROM EATING DISORDER AND TRAUMA TO THE STRONGEST WOMAN IN CROATIA

Milijana de Mori

You are not supposed to read these words because they were written by a former child refugee, bulimic teenager and deeply broken and hopeless young woman. At the darkest moments of my life, I had no reason to live and so many to just leave this world behind. But here I am telling you that positive transformation is possible, that a great life can be created and lived.

Positive transformation starts with curiosity and empowering questions.
Replacing: *Why me? Why is life so hard?*
With: *How can life be better?*
What can I do to be happier?
Who can I ask for guidance?
What skills do I need to overcome this?

These questions are fuelled by core beliefs about life and yourself. Your beliefs are your absolute truths and run the show (your habits, emotions, decisions, behaviours). For example, if you strongly believe 'people can't be trusted', you will only notice and have relationships with those who can confirm your 'truth'; you won't even see or be attracted to those who don't match this belief. What you expect and deeply believe in you'll experience more of.

The solution: When you change your questions and inner beliefs, your behaviours and experience will change.

Language upgrade

One of my first aha-moments came when hearing that when we improve the way we talk to ourselves we can change how we feel. It's moving from complaining and victimhood to choices and possibilities. I had no idea that I could be gentle and nice towards myself. Only criticism felt like home and the belief that 'when I'm perfect I'll be loved' drove my life.

You are always in your own company, so why not speak nicely with yourself? Why not be your own biggest supporter? It feels so much better and doesn't depend on others. It's taking your own power back and giving yourself what you need. No one needs to hear you talking to yourself nicely.

Language upgrades will spark the positive transformation and are key to keeping those positive changes. Sometimes after reading books and attending workshops we feel on a high and everything is awesome, but shortly after we move back into our limiting behaviours or habits – that's where language comes in. When you actively use empowering language, moving forward becomes easier and long-lasting.

Disempowering / Victim Language	Empowering Language / Choice
I can't	I won't / I decided not to
I should	I could / I will
It's not my fault	I'm totally responsible
It's a problem	It's an opportunity
I'm never satisfied	I want to learn and grow
Life's a struggle	Life's an adventure
I hope	I know / I firmly believe
If only	Next time
What will I do?	I know I can handle it
It's terrible	It's a learning experience / Let's look for solutions
	I am
	I can
	I will
	I create
	I choose
	I make up
	I like / love

"*I am*" is the most powerful statement because it refers to your identity, to who you are. Use it to your advantage and choose empowerment that can sound like: "I am a great person. I am always on time. I am living courageously."

Turn a curse into a gift

Know where you are (point A – often point of pain) and where you want to be (point B – desirable outcome). Self-knowledge enables you to create massive transformations in any area of your life. This will require honesty and courage (*definition: the ability to undertake an overwhelming difficulty or pain despite the imminent and unavoidable presence of fear*). Only when it feels uncomfortable and only when you feel fear do you have the opportunity to demonstrate courage.

The difference between a coward and a hero is that the hero moves forward and does what needs to be done despite the fear. The coward lets the fear stop them and dictate their life.

I was bulimic for 13 years and it was the source of my biggest shame. I considered it a curse and sign of weakness. My sporting and academic achievements meant nothing because I had this dark secret for so many years.

Ten years ago, I overcame my eating disorder. It started with the inner work, moving into self-care, standing up for myself and taking charge of my life.

Today the old curse is my biggest gift because I help individuals worldwide overcome their eating disorders. I truly understand their journey and they trust me – I lived the same secrets; the perfectionism; the belief that only when I looked a certain way would I be accepted; and the questions: "What's wrong with me? Why can't I control this?"

What is your biggest pain? Let it unfold as your own gift. I promise you, our biggest and most painful lessons are our biggest and most powerful contributions.

Find your tribe

You are not alone. There are so many ready to show you the way, to support you. It's your initial action and their reaction. I firmly believe in results, so choose someone who's living what you are trying to achieve.

Yes, you can do it alone, but with someone in your corner it's much easier and more fun.

Elegant, graceful, purposeful responsibility

You have arrived at the right place. You are on time. Now is the moment of possibilities and decisions.

Taking this book into your hands means you are ready for the next step, for the transformation.

Taking responsibility for all areas of your life as they are now will give you the freedom and opportunity to mould it. Your relationships, career, finances, emotions, health – it's in your hands. Claiming this will change everything. Blaming no one from this moment will create empowerment.

Purposeful and elegant responsibility is a daily choice and you can start with empowering questions, by writing and talking in a way that supports you, by noticing where growth is possible and where you can ask for guidance. You are ready.

MILIJANA DE MORI

Having overcome her eating disorder, war trauma and low self-esteem, Milijana de Mori now coaches clients from all around the world to overcome their eating disorders and trauma, for good.

Before becoming a full-time coach, she won gold medals in three sports: kick-boxing, Olympic weightlifting and powerlifting (setting national records in Croatia and Western Australia) and held the title Strongest Woman in Croatia before she retired from competitive sport. She also coaches athletes and professionals to reach their best results in high-stress situations.

Milijana is facilitating and presenting at retreats and workshops in Europe, USA and Australia. She has a Bachelor of Business, is an HNLP master practitioner and has completed several other coaching programmes (EFT, matrix reimprinting and reiki).

She has lived in Germany and Australia and now resides in Split, Croatia, with her husband and two cats, where she's finishing her book *How Not to be a Jealous and Controlling B!tch.*

milijanademori.com
www.instagram.com/milijana.de.mori
www.fb.com/coach.Milijana
www.linkedin.com/in/milijana-de-mori

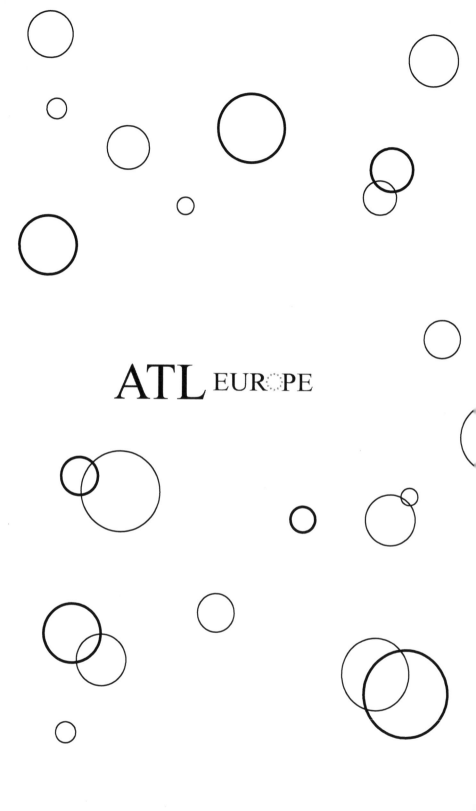

Chapter 10

FINDING YOUR SOUL PURPOSE

Marie Diamond

On 22 September 1978, a truck nearly killed me. It hit me, and I flew more than 50 metres on pebble stones. When the ambulance came, they declared me dead and covered my body with white fabric. This happened close to my home on my way from school.

When my parents arrived at the scene, my mother insisted that they try to revive me again. In the ambulance, I had an out-of-body experience: I saw a very cute blond male nurse reviving me, and my mother next to me crying. Then I went into a very beautiful space of light and there were all beings of light present. I remember them telling me: "You need to go back. Your task is to enlighten more than 500 million people." I woke up several days later with the words in my head. I was 15.

As I lay in hospital, I contemplated this sentence. What did it mean? 'Enlightening'. I had never heard of this word. I concluded that it meant to make a positive difference in the life of 500 million people. But how? I had no idea how to start.

I found out that I needed plastic surgery as the skin of my face was completely gone. I refused the procedure and said to my mother: "I will heal myself." I started putting my hands on my face, transmitting light and focusing on creating new skin. Two weeks later I was able to go back to school with a completely healed face.

Then I knew that if I could make a difference in myself with that light, that I had a chance to bring light to 500 million people.

From that moment on, I have asked myself every morning: "I am here to enlighten more than 500 million people. God or the universe, show me how I can make this happen today."

I started in my own school and community, trying to make a difference by being more grateful to the teachers, helping students; becoming engaged in social projects; starting up a meditation group in school; volunteering at the Catholic church; writing letters for Amnesty International; marching on the streets to free victims of dictators; leading young people in a Catholic youth movement; and sharing my poetry, music, and dance in front of thousands.

When I was 19, I decided to study law so that I could work for the United Nations or as a politician to make a difference for millions. After working for the Belgian and European governments for five years, I decided that it was not the right way to enlighten millions of people.

At 30, I started teaching meditation, the path to enlightenment and how to release your inner blockages through the Inner Diamond Meditation. Within one year, I was reaching thousands of people in Belgium. I knew I was on the right track.

I also started teaching feng shui as I knew it is hard to reach enlightenment when your home has a lower vibration. Diamond Feng Shui was created to enlighten your environment.

Then at the end of the 90s, I received the inner guidance that I needed to really expand into millions. I started teaching my work in the US, where I knew my impact would be greater.

I used the law of attraction to attract millions on my path. Every day I would ask the same question: "Show me how." I was guided all the time through the light. One morning in 2002, while staying in San Francisco, I received an inner message: "You have to live here in three weeks".

With my family, I moved to the US and then a sequence of situations unfolded that brought me in contact with Jack Canfield. He invited me to be a founding member of the Transformational Leadership Council in 2003. There, I was filmed by Rhonda Byrne and I became the only European transformational teacher in the movie and best-selling book, *The Secret*. This phenomenon has reached more than 500 million people alone.

My question to you is: "What is your soul purpose?" Perhaps you know already, and you just need to really start focusing on it. Ask every morning before you start your busy day: "Show me how to unfold my purpose". It is possible that you are not aware of it yet and that you need more clarity. Ask for clarity from your soul about your path.

I believe that every living soul has a purpose. The purpose is to grow spiritually and to become a better human being and share this in service with others. It is possible that you are unfolding your purpose through your professional activities, your family, your friends, your religious or spiritual community or your passions.

But I am asking you: Are you aware of it? Do you fulfil your purpose with intention? Are you just living a busy life without conscious awareness of the impact you are making? Put a number on the conscious difference you wish to create in the world and the law of attraction will direct you to opportunities and possibilities that are bigger than you can imagine. Do not ask yourself how that is going to be possible. Believe that God or the universe can see beyond your limiting perspective and belief system.

How could I have known at 15 how to reach millions of people through a book and a movie called *The Secret*, teaching millions of people about the law of attraction, meditation, feng shui and dowsing and even founding ATL Europe and writing this chapter for you? I didn't, but I knew that God or the Universe had a bigger plan for me than I could ever have imagined. I know there is a bigger plan for you too. Tune into it, ask for guidance and let it unfold.

MARIE DIAMOND

Marie Diamond is a globally renowned transformational teacher, leader, motivational speaker and international bestselling author of *Transform your Life* and *The Energy Number Book*, creator of the Diamond Feng Shui, Diamond Dowsing and Inner Diamond Meditation programmes. She is also the only European star in the worldwide phenomenon, *The Secret*.

She uses her extraordinary knowledge of energy, quantum physics, the law of attraction, and ancient wisdom like meditation, feng shui and dowsing to support individuals, organisations and corporations to transform their success, financial situation, relationships, motivation and inspiration.

As founder of the Institute for Global Enlightened Leadership, Marie helps leaders to create a bigger enlightened impact. She was a founding member of the Transformational Leadership council, and also started the Association of Transformational Leaders for Europe (ATL Europe), with members in more than 22 countries.

www.MarieDiamond.com
www.linkedin.com/in/mariediamond/
www.facebook.com/mariediamondfans/
www.instagram.com/mariediamond8
twitter.com/mariediamond888

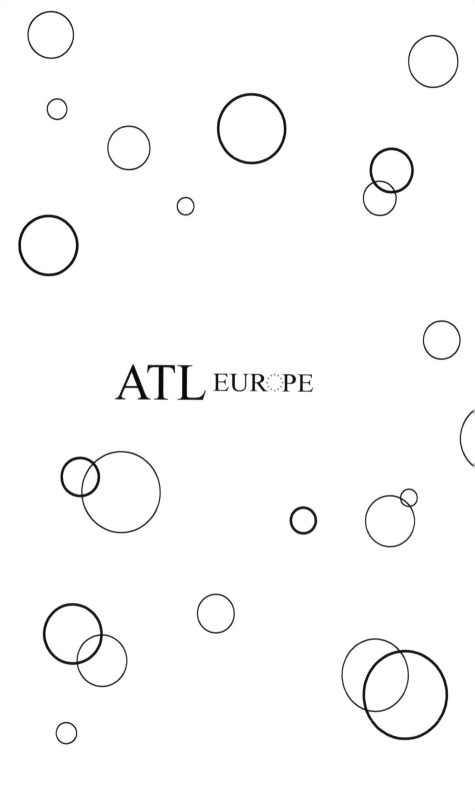

ATL EUR⬡PE

Chapter 11

TRANSFORMATIONS FOR FINANCIAL FREEDOM

Bindar Dosanjh

Imagine having cash coming in your bank account every month for the rest of your life when you did the work just once. Or having a healthy pension pot so you never worry about your retirement? When you retire, will you have the time to relax and enjoy life? Will you have enough money to fund that lifestyle?

Today I am a multi-award-winning property developer, property strategist, mentor, trainer and lawyer, with a portfolio worth several million pounds, achieved as a single parent with a full-time job. But I became a property multimillionaire by accident.

I was brought up in a strict traditional Indian family with very little money. I wasn't encouraged to have a career but was prepared for marriage. Men were the breadwinners and women looked after the children and the home. I didn't know any different so complied. At 20, I had an arranged marriage and moved to London to live with my husband's parents. My salary went directly to my mother-in-law, who controlled the household finances: to me, this was normal.

My marriage broke down, leaving me alone with my nine-month-old daughter and thinking: "What do I do?" There was a recession, and interest rates were at an all-time high. The mortgage interest rate on my home was an incredible 15%. My secretarial salary was £7,500 a year and I just couldn't make ends meet. In September

1991, I queued for hours with my daughter at the local authority benefit office, desperate for money, only to be told I'd not paid enough in National Insurance contributions.

This was a turning point in my life: I decided never to rely on anyone else financially again. So reluctantly I became a landlady, renting rooms in my house just to survive. As a legal secretary, I had often known I could do a better job than my boss. I believed that being the boss would solve all my money problems, so I started studying part-time to become a lawyer. It took me over seven years to complete. Many times, I wanted to give up, as I was constantly exhausted being a mum as well as studying and working full-time.

This was when I first heard the negative voices of others. Some said I didn't have the ability to be a lawyer, others that I wasn't good enough and would fail, and others that I should give up and be satisfied with what I had. My first transformation was to fully believe in me. I then made a promise to my daughter to provide her with a better life; I was determined to keep it. I qualified as a lawyer on 15 November 1996: one of the proudest moments of my life. It brings tears to my eyes when I realise my achievement. While I started a new path, an old path ended with the receipt of my final divorce papers on the very same day.

Now studying was hard work, but frankly, proving myself to my bosses was even harder; dealing with targets and demonstrating I was equal to, if not better than, my male colleagues was harder. Then came my second accidental move into property. I needed to move closer to work, but realised that emotionally I couldn't sell my matrimonial home, so I rented it out to buy a second home.

It was 2004; I had money but no spare time. I was busy climbing the legal corporate ladder. This is when I made one of my biggest mistakes, which later became another transformation. I saw a newspaper advert saying: "Become an armchair investor." The investment company helped me refinance my properties, and then sold me properties all over the UK and Spain. Their promises did not materialise and I lost more than £150,000 as I gave them my financial power. But worse than that, I lost my confidence.

Now I could either make these properties work, or declare myself bankrupt. The latter option would mean I could no longer practice as a lawyer, so I had to make the deals work. But my debt increased and even compounded: rather than these properties feeding me, my hard-earned salary fed them.

Just as I hit rock bottom, I had my second transformation. I got educated about property investing and wealth creation, and got a property investing mentor. This turned my life around for my daughter and me.

I believe everyone should invest. You cannot leave your financial future to chance or rely on others to handle it. Put yourself first!

Financial issues and crises show up when you least expect them – are you prepared for them? I was certainly not prepared for the next recession and lost my role as a senior departmental head. I avoided a financial crisis by paying my bills with the income from my accidental hobby of investing.

I set up my own law firm helping vulnerable victims of family breakdowns. It was a great success, winning recognition and many awards. But life threw me another curve ball. At 5am I was woken by noises in my bedroom. Opening my eyes, I saw a man standing over me wearing a balaclava and gloves. His threatening whisper said: "I'm going to kill you!" I believed I was going to die. There were two men in my room: one guarding the door, while the other filled bags with my precious possessions. They took everything of value, including my ability to serve others. I could no longer deal with my clients' cases, as I was traumatised emotionally.

Reluctantly I closed my law firm, and then had my third transformation. I turned my part-time hobby of property investing into my full-time passion by inspiring others that if I can do it, so can they. Today, I help beginners to property investing, as they get the biggest transformations; from fearful to fearless. I also founded a women-only networking group, the Female Property Alliance, dedicated to advancing the success, collaboration and connections of female property investors in the UK.

My transformations show others how to create their own choices, a work-life balance and freedom to live their desired lifestyle. Property investing is a vehicle enabling you to be passionate about your life.

My transformations involved five lessons:

1. **Believe in yourself.** Never allow other people's negative opinions to affect your judgment; follow your gut instinct.

2. **Connect with like-minded people**. Those on the same journey share in your dreams and hold you accountable, pushing you to the next level, and never hold you back.

3. **Keep your financial power.** Never give away your financial power to anyone, you take responsibility as no one will look after it like you.

4. **Stay focused on your goal.** Know your end result and remain determined to achieve it by never giving up.

5. **Ask an expert.** Never rely on amateurs to provide professional advice; pick your team wisely as they will keep you safe and accelerate your success.

BINDAR DOSANJH

Bindar Dosanjh is a multi-award-winning property investor, property strategist, mentor, trainer and lawyer. An acclaimed international speaker, she inspires thousands of people each year to get into property investing to control their financial destiny with her message of: "If I can do it, so can you."

Bindar now has a property portfolio worth several million pounds. She has done it the hard way as a single parent with a full-time job. Brought up in a strict traditional Indian family with very little money, she overcame many obstacles including racial abuse and six-figure financial losses.

She is now financially free and living her dream lifestyle. She lives her mission every day by empowering, educating and enabling others to achieve what she has done, and believing there is a property strategy that works for everyone.

"You don't have to be passionate about property investing, but you certainly need to be passionate about your life. Financial transformations work only with the right wealth mindset: which I have the gift to help you achieve."

www.smartcorewealth.com
www.femalepropertyalliance.co.uk
www.facebook.com/FemalePropertyAlliance/
www.facebook.com/bindardosanjh/
www.linkedin.com/in/bindardosanjhproperty/

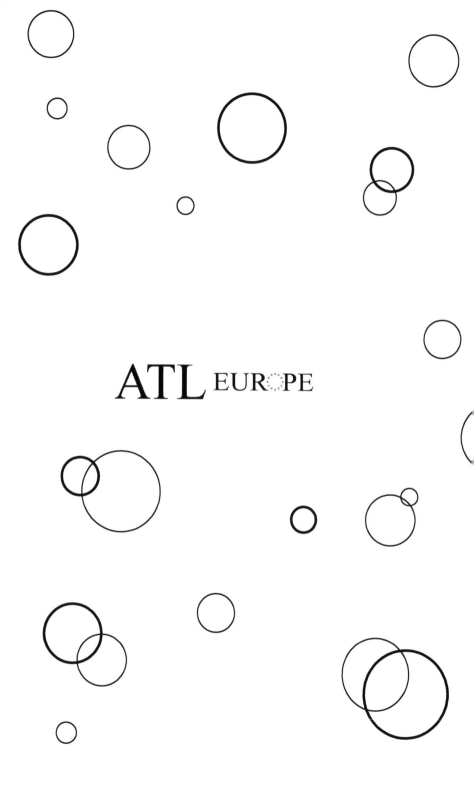

Chapter 12

WOMEN, WILDERNESS, ADVENTURE

Catherine Edsell

"In the wilderness, and when faced with physical and mental challenges you tend to feed off other people's strength, experiences and struggles. No one has any expectations of you, they are just glad to be in your company." These were the words of Fiona, a woman on *The Matriarch Adventure*, one of the transformational adventures I have created.

And Fiona was right. This is what I witnessed – a community of women, of different ages, from different countries, who, a few days previously, had not known each other, but were now lifelong friends.

I am, by profession, an expedition leader, but I have wrestled with the fact that for me, motherhood has been the hardest challenge I have ever had to face. I was under the illusion that I could just strap my baby to my back and carry on. I'd seen women all over the world do it – how hard could it be? It turned out to be much harder than it looked, on so many levels, and when my second daughter was born, and my first was exhibiting developmental issues, my world really closed in.

One year, for my birthday, my brother sent me a card with the words: "I wanted to go out and change the world, but I couldn't find a babysitter." emblazoned across the front. I laughed and then I cried, never had words been truer. I didn't know exactly how I would change the world; I didn't even have a plan, but the feeling of being trapped by my situation was so great that I couldn't bear it. This drive to overcome my own experience, which I did, over time, led me to offer an opportunity for liberation to others in a similar situation.

Women today are so separated from each other. Mothers at home alone with small children often suffer extreme bouts of depression, as do mothers whose children have flown the nest, as do women who can't have children. The statistics are that one in four women will suffer some form of depression during their lives.

We live in an isolated society, and through my travels around the world I have seen how impoverished we are because of this. Without a community surrounding us, holding us accountable, supporting us and encouraging us, without communal activities, such as cooking together, making things together, sharing the childcare, spending time in another people's company, we quickly start to close down, to retreat, and suffer silently, alone.

For me, expeditions are my reset button. On expedition, I remember that I can cope with pretty much anything, like landslides and volcanoes erupting – at home, I have been known to get stressed if the dishwasher doesn't drain properly. On expedition, I become fit and strong by using my body in a *real* way, walking, climbing, swimming. I find that I worry less: it's as though my physical senses become so overwhelmed, my mind clears. That's me – happy.

The Matriarch Adventure was born of a desire to share the joys I experience on expedition with others, to allow women to push their own boundaries. When you discover what you are capable of, rediscover what you may have forgotten about yourself, immerse yourself in awe-inspiring nature, there's a shift in perspective, in your confidence in yourself. You are inspired and return home ready to take on new challenges.

It is not that I don't think men should have adventures: they should, and they do. It's just that in my experience, as a woman and a mother, I notice the limitations we create around what we allow ourselves to do. Are you always compromising, multitasking, taking the slack, holding the fort? That's all great, except if you are doing that *all* the time. Why not give yourself a few days, once in a while, to go off on your own, to reconnect with yourself, to challenge yourself physically, to marvel at the wonders of nature, to learn, to grow. It's also important to strip away, to get back to basics, to clear your thinking, and perhaps even change your mindset. Even just thinking about this, you may meet amazing resistance, even if it is what you actually really need.

The women who sign up are not habitual adventurers: they are housewives, mothers, ordinary women who seize this opportunity to step out of their everyday lives and have an incredible adventure.

I came to this conclusion, and this is my transformational lesson to you:

> *Adventure in remote and extreme wilderness environments with other women, has a powerful, transformative effect, quickly stripping away the non-essential trappings of modern life in all its guises, (be they physical, social, or otherwise), replacing them with integrity, clarity and sisterhood. This new paradigm allows you to rediscover what it is to be a confident, self-reliant woman, and to return to your everyday lives supported and empowered.*

Can you imagine, 10 days, 10 women, in the Namibian wilderness, tracking elusive desert elephants (the most iconic matriarchs there are), having an adventure, dawn yoga under huge flame-red skies, inspiration round a camp fire, sleeping out under a myriad of stars, meeting Namibian women and hearing their story – and all else that expedition life has to offer.

There is nothing more restorative than real immersion in true wilderness without all the 'stuff' we think we need – just expansive, blue skies, the sun on your face, the earth under your feet, the wind in your hair, a group of new friends walking beside you in the silence, and perhaps even an elephant wandering quietly by. Just close your eyes, and imagine…

Now get out there!

CATHERINE EDSELL

Catherine Edsell is an adventurer and global expedition leader. An avid naturalist, she combines her passion for adventure and effective conservation through independent and collaborative expedition work in the most remote areas of the world.

She is a trained PADI divemaster, reef check trainer, coral reef ecologist, mountain leader, jungle trainer and yoga teacher, with 20 years' experience working in all manner of terrains, often with her children in tow. Inspired by her immersion in stunning natural habitats, Catherine is now leading a series of transformative adventures solely for women.

Through travel to extreme wilderness locations, in close proximity to wildlife, Catherine designs expeditions that open up her world of adventure to any woman who wishes to seize the opportunity to step out of their comfort zone, push their own mental and physical boundaries, and in doing so, rediscover themselves.

info@cathadventure.com
www.cathadventure.com
twitter.com/cathadventure
www.instagram.com/cathadventure
www.facebook.com/catherine.edsell
www.facebook.com/matriarchadventure/
www.facebook.com/thebluemoonadventure
www.linkedin.com/in/catherine-edsell-frgs

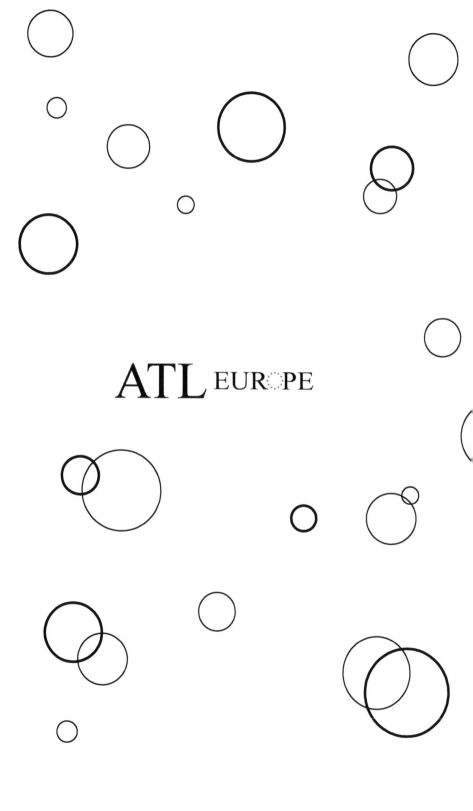

Chapter 13

BREATHING, RHYTHM, DISSOLVING STRESS

Viola Edward

Stress is a state of inner anxiety occurring in many aspects of our lives. It triggers processes of non-communication, hindering productivity, creativity and intimacy. All of us can be affected by this 'condition'. Symptoms of stress, such as bad moods, prolonged tiredness, anxiety, lack of motivation and negative vision, are common in today's world. A major obstacle to healing this 'illness' lies in the fact that stress continuously feeds back on itself. Once it is present in the organism, its effect becomes a cause. It is important to differentiate between what I call 'creative tension' and 'real stress'.

Creative tension is a stressful situation where we retain a certain control, such as in the practice of sport or the organisation of a wedding. Real stress appears in situations where we have no control over the event, as in an accident, a natural disaster or an economic crisis. One of the most devastating physical effects of stress is the subconscious inhibition of breathing.

With the repetition of stressful situations, these dysfunctional breathing habits become chronic and can lead to frustration, lack of purpose and difficulty in expressing love and gratitude, all of which will affect our joy in life. To liberate ourselves from these effects, the study and practice of healthy breathing techniques is an excellent starting point.

Breathing is a life-sustaining activity that we begin to practise instinctively from the moment we are born and continues uninterrupted until the moment we die. The continuous rhythm of our respiration is such a familiar practice to us that, most of our lives, we are even unaware of our participation in this vital action. Remember that, although we can survive for many days without food and not quite so long without water, if we are prevented from breathing, most of us will be dead within three or four minutes.

This is how fundamental the breathing process is to our wellbeing. Let us take a closer look at the dynamics of the breathing process. Singers and wind instrument players, among others, are always conscious of breathing, as their music depends on being able to deliver a continuous flow of breath across the vocal chords or through their musical instruments.

Athletes depend on powerful breathing rhythms to be able to deliver high levels of oxygen to their performing muscles. The air that we inhale into our lungs contains a percentage of oxygen and when this oxygen content comes into contact with the blood circulating in the spongy tissues of our lungs, it is absorbed into the bloodstream. The steady pumping of our heart transports this oxygen-rich blood to our brain and to the muscles and organs of our bodies, where the oxygen is consumed in an energy-supplying mission.

When we are working hard, our hearts beat faster, and we breathe more strongly to supply the increase in energy required by our bodies. In a healthy body, this biological breathing dynamic manages itself naturally and instinctively without the requirement of any conscious intervention.

We are however, capable of intervening in this natural sequence by *intentionally modifying the character of our breathing rhythms*. For example, if we choose to breathe more strongly than usual while remaining physically inactive, we influence the natural equilibrium of the supply and demand of oxygen, creating a higher than usual level of energy throughout our bodies. Research and practical experimentation with the effects of unusual body energy levels has led to the development of many physical and spiritual practices that we find in various disciplines of healing and in the martial arts.

Both ancestral and modern practices acknowledge the importance of breathing in processes of transformation. There are various types of stress and my reference here is to stress produced by experiences that were neither accepted nor integrated into our life, developing subsequently into traumas. These were probably situations generated by fear, shame, anger, loss, or other limiting emotions and were experienced at an age when we were unable to manage the event, or the perception of the event. The situation could have occurred in a moment of extreme vulnerability, creating a wound that couldn't heal completely. To survive the pain, we learned how to create a variety of defence mechanisms, but the wound remained there, getting deeper, becoming chronic and sometimes extremely acute.

Following a therapeutic journey of understanding and healing the wounds of traumatic experiences is a must for a return to balanced life. The choice of using energy work such as breathwork coaching, alongside the psychotherapeutic process, is very powerful. As holistic beings, we need to heal in all our dimensions (body, mind, emotion, spirit/meaning). Such healing processes can include learning to express, to feel and to understand.

Through releasing, resolving and transforming, I learn to accept and integrate, benefiting then from the joy and the bliss of the intimacy with myself and my partner. Each healed wound may leave a scar, a testimony of the journey of healing. We can even be proud of them. When those wounds were still open and unattended, an accumulation of demanding situations or some new and acute stress could lead us to a breakdown. However, once the wounds have been attended to and have healed, even though we are carrying the scars, when similar situations reappear, we will be able to break through them and learn from the experience. This is what I call 'emotional freedom'.

Relaxation and stress cannot exist at the same time in the same place, and since breathing consciously leads us into relaxation, the more time we practice conscious breathing, the less time we will be subject to harmful stress.

There are seven fundamental elements to transform stress:

1. Breathe consciously, being aware of your thinking.

2. Inhale, recognising who you are.

3. Exhale, letting go of what you no longer need.

4. Be present, asking clearly for what you want.

5. Accept and forgive, giving with love and generosity.

6. Keep on improving and expanding with gratitude.

7. Open your heart, letting love in and taking care of your surroundings.

VIOLA EDWARD

Viola Edward is a psychotherapist and breathwork pioneer with over 25 years' experience. A leader with individual and corporate clients, she specialises in stress management, training in breathwork coaching, feminine energy and relationships. She is the co-founder of Kayana International Breathwork and author of two books: *Breathing the Rhythm of Success* and *Who Makes the Bed?*

Viola has mentored thousands of people in 17 countries towards achieving their full potential, using her practical methods to unlock their hidden possibilities. She speaks English, Spanish and Arabic.

Viola is a multi-award-winner and in July 2018 she was awarded an honorary doctorate by the Academy of Universal Global Peace under affiliation of the United Nations for her humanitarian work and leadership.

Viola has been an immigrant many times in her life. She is Venezuelan with Middle-Eastern origins. In 2002, she moved to Cyprus for love.

www.violaedward.com
www.facebook.com/ViolaEdwardMentor
www.linkedin.com/in/Viola-Edward
www.instagram.com/viola_edward_official
twitter.com/ViolaEdeG

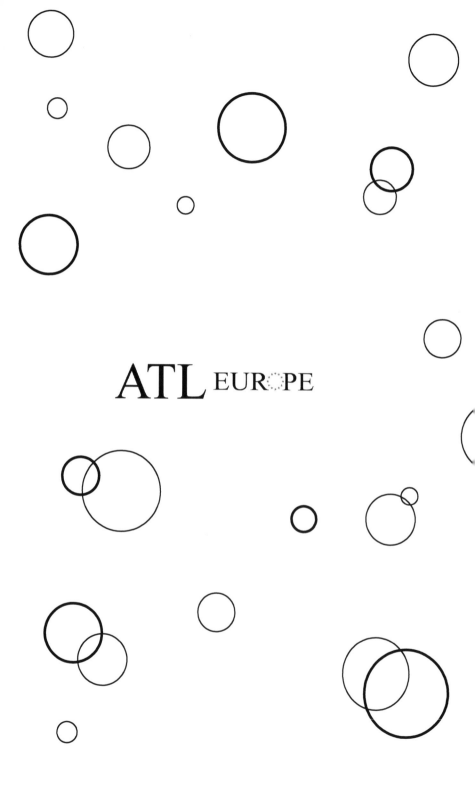

Chapter 14

HOW YOUR SOFTWARE RUNS YOUR LIFE

Ivan Faes

Why did you pick up this book? There could be a bunch of reasons.

One thing I know for sure: you're looking for something. Something you might not be able to put your finger on, something you can't fully explain, but you feel it. Something is off, something is changing; your life just isn't the same as it used to be. What's up with the world, maybe your world? A search that for most people starts outside ourselves.

Let's pretend that today is your birthday. So what happened on that day years ago?

You entered this world, after being protected and nourished for nine months in your mother's womb. A lot had happened: you'd started from just a few cells, and you'd grown into a baby with millions of cells.

You knew very little of this world. You got just a few survival tactics and you were fully dependent on your parents.

Did you know that humans have the longest period of all animals to bring up their offspring?

Our brain needs roughly 25 years to mature. It used to be believed that, after that time, the brain couldn't be modified. That belief has been debunked with the discovery of neuroplasticity (the ability to change throughout life). All good, but what does it mean to us? What's in it for me? Well, I believe that the brain pretty much works like a computer.

Like every computer, it runs software, and this software controls our destiny – the output from the system. Mmm – software, you say? Yes – software.

So where did this software come from? It's been installed.

Let's go back to the baby version of our species. The initial software is programmed for survival and includes five reflexes. You'll find them on Google if you want to go deeper into this.

This is where it gets interesting. We'll assume in this chapter that the rest of the software is installed. So how does this software get on the system? As babies grow and explore, they learn things – and what they learn is information provided to them – information from parents, family, friends and society. Information from experience, especially emotional experiences like trauma. As the brain initially doesn't logically understand what things mean, it attaches a meaning to an event.

These meanings or interpretations are seen as the truth, especially before the age of six.

One of my coaching clients told me that he didn't understand what was going on. He's a good-looking, smart, bright and sociable person. Yet at the age of 32 he'd never had a serious love relationship. He told me that every time he got close to someone, he felt like a switch went off in his head and he turned cold on them.

This intrigued me, and we quickly traced it to an event that happened in his childhood. At one point, he was reaching out to pet a dog, with all his love and joy. Only the dog didn't respond in kind and bit him. So, his brain, his computer, installed "Send out love and joy to people and you get bitten – you feel pain!"

The brain learns super quickly when this happens before the age of six, which it did. His whole life, he had avoided getting too close to someone – to avoid pain.

Never understanding it was just some bad software running in his brain.

Bad in the sense it was not serving a 32-year-old man. Good in that, yes, at one point it helped him as a kid to avoid getting hurt. Which brings us to the primary function of our brain/computer: its sole interest is keeping you alive. A lot, if not all, of what the software is doing is keeping you from harm.

"Is all the software designed to keep us from harm?"

No. There's some software designed to make you feel better in the short term. This is why addictions are another key in the software: you have this impulse: "I feel a bit down." The answer from your brain? "Let's get some sugar. You'll feel better!" This is an excellent short-term strategy, but it's fundamentally flawed in the long term: most of the time, addictions require a bigger and bigger dose to have an effect as the brain adjusts.

"Yeah, yeah, I know all this." Sure, you do – but common knowledge isn't always common practice. As you started out, initially there's not that much software installed, and by the age of 35, up to 95% of our thoughts and software are firmly in place. Meaning only 5% will be looked at consciously. "Ninety-five per cent, you say?" Yes!

If you want a better life, more joy, more love, more money, better relationships, you will have to go on a quest to find out: "What software am I running? Is this software serving me or 'surviving' me?"

In society, rumours spread that we have no control of our destiny, no control over how we feel. No control of outside events. Well, no control of events is true. You do, however, control the software that will process the event and give it meaning. The meaning your software puts on it will define how you feel. Ultimately you feel the way your 95% automated system decided in a fraction of a second.

It's time to understand, and to start to feel that the one in charge ultimately is you.

As a high-performance coach, I help people to discover the software that runs their mind, to change parts of that software, to reinstall and clean up so they can get the most out of their life.

I believe we all have innate gifts and that there is more than enough joy, love, and money to go around. Surrounding myself with the best mentors and trainers in the fields of high performance, peak performance and habit-forming has taught me that transformation comes from within. Understand that we all want to be loved. That love starts with you – yes, *you*. When people ask me: "Ivan, from your vast experience and training, what is the one thing that would change my life?", my answer is: "I'll give you two: love yourself, and trust yourself."

When you do that – like, really *feel* it – you've discovered the gas and oil to run the engine. Get that engine running, and you'll do and be whatever it is you want your legacy to be. If I can in any way help you in that legacy, it is my honour to serve and do my part in helping the planet to move to a higher state of consciousness. Or to put it in software terms – the next release.

IVAN FAES

Ivan Faes started his career in IT – aged just 18, he deployed infrastructure for companies such as BMW, Toyota, SkyNet, and Relay (press).

He is fascinated by the 'working of things', this enables him to analyse the process and see the core of the problem. This skill to see things, not only how they are, but also how they could be, is a massive driver. It pushes him to be a better version of himself, and to teach this to others.

He trained and studied with the industry's best, Tony Robbins, Brendon Burchard, and Richard Bandler, to name a few.

Ivan is a High Performance coach, Breakthrough specialist and on a mission to empower High Performers to leave a Legacy. He helps them transform themselves, their teams, their customers and ultimately the world. "Legends aren't born, they are built."

transformwithin.com
www.facebook.com/TransformWithinCom
www.instagram.com/transformwithincom
www.linkedin.com/in/ivanfaes
twitter.com/WithinTransform

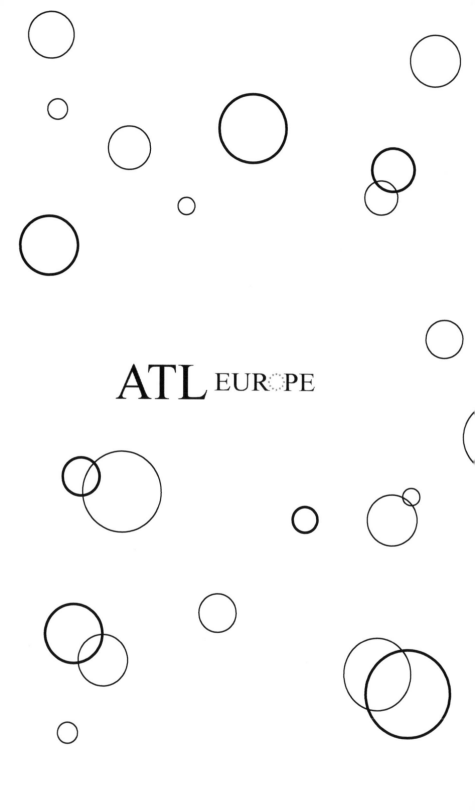

Chapter 15

HOW TO CHANGE 500 LIVES

Carole Fossey

If you had been with me on Monday, 11 June 2018, you would have seen me looking forward to a well-earned day off. I had just returned from coaching a bunch of 'elite' speakers on high-level public speaking skills over the previous seven days and was looking forward to relaxing and absorbing the week's successes and learnings.

After a day of cleaning and house tidying – I love my husband and son very much for their many beautiful qualities: sadly housework is not one of them – I had just sat down on one of three black leather couches in the lounge at 4pm with a cup of tea. The phone rang. "Oh no, who is that?", I thought, looking at my phone. I thought it was a random Facebook connection who might be a spammer and nearly didn't pick up. Then I recalled a message the week before from a lady called Rukhiya Budden, whom I had coached at a previous public speaking event. I had asked her to call back this week.

Groaning slightly inside, I answered.

"Carole, I'm so sorry to trouble you, I don't really know why I am calling but I felt compelled to call you. I felt like we made a strong connection at the event and I remembered what you taught me. You remember how I was raised in an orphanage in Kenya, and I wanted to start a charity to get children *out* of orphanages and *into* loving homes? Well, I decided to team up with a charity that already does that – it's called Hope and Homes for Children. It just popped up on my Instagram and I knew it was the right charity."

"Rukhiya, that's fantastic news and yes of course I remember coaching you. How can I help?"

"Well Carole, here's the thing. The charity took me back to Kenya and filmed my life story, and they have created an event at Abbey Road Studios where they have given me six minutes to speak from stage and raise as much money as possible for the charity. Can I read you my speech?"

So Rukhiya read me her speech. She was like a newsreader – dispassionately telling me the terrible facts of her life in the orphanage. I knew this could be a truly powerful piece, if we could just transform it into a story.

"That's great Rukhiya. Are you happy for me to change this? I would like to rewrite it. How long have we got?"

"Well, the event is on Wednesday and the speech has already been signed off by the charity."

"OK, give me an hour Rukhiya, I will rewrite it and then we can jump on Skype and practise how to present it."

An hour later you will find me on Skype reading Rukhiya the new words. She became very emotional "Oh my God, Carole, that's it. That is *exactly* what I was feeling: you have captured it perfectly."

Monday night was spent coaching this newly created story. Only it wasn't newly created – it was *her* story – just relived, rather than told. I fell into bed, tired but happy that she was happy. The new wording was signed off the next day.

On Thursday, 14 June Rukhiya rang me. To say she was excited would have been to do her no justice at all. She almost screamed down the phone – "Thank you thank you thank you thank you!

We *did* it! I can't believe it. I got a standing ovation. And we raised £600,000 on the night. That means *you* have helped take 500 children out of orphanages, Carole. What a legacy. What a difference you made. I don't know how to thank you. You need to write all my future speeches – ha ha!"

"I'm so glad to have been able to help, Rukhiya – but *you* did it. You were the one who took action and got in touch with the charity. You were the one brave enough to stand up on stage in front of hundreds of strangers and bare your soul. I'm so proud of you."

People sometimes ask me how I manage to fit everything in. I run a busy growing social media company of (currently) 14 people, a recruitment training company, a women's Mastermind Group and networking company (Leading Women in Business). I write business and children's books and create three blogs a week. I speak from stage whenever I can and travel as much as possible, and I am also a mum and big family person.

There are times when it doesn't all fit perfectly and I could give up the public speaking coaching – as the least 'well paid' of everything I do – which would give me a bit more time. However, I never will. And that's because of the joy it brings me personally and the way I can help people to touch hearts and minds through the power of words, and the delivery of those words. Nothing reaches people more powerfully than a beautifully crafted, truthful and emotional message, delivered with passion and poise – whether that is in a blog, on social media or on video where you can reach millions – or of course – from stage.

The knowledge that I have helped, in any way, to take one child out of an orphanage would be wonderful. To have been given an opportunity to help 500 is an incredible privilege and something I will keep in my heart for all my days.

Don't you find that it is the things you do for no financial reward that ultimately bring you the most reward? I've learned there is no value in playing small or asking: "Who am I to... ?"

You have unique skills and insights, and, as my mentor says, if you do not share them with the world then you are being selfish. You never know the impact you have on another. So, don't play small. Play all out. Go change the world!

CAROLE FOSSEY

Carole Fossey is an author, public speaker, small business coach and founder of carolefossey.com and strategysocialmedia.co.uk. She recently won Global Coach of the Year at the Professional Speakers Academy.

Carole's career began in HR, followed by success in sales and training. She started her own recruitment agency in 2001, working with companies like Visa, along with many small and medium enterprises.

Ahead of the curve, Carole founded Strategy Social Media and developed the S.M.A.R.T. Social System. She is also the author of *The Book on Recruitment*, *Your Business Network* and children's book *Princess Phoebe Wants A Sister*.

Carole@carolefossey.com
twitter.com/CaroleFossey
twitter.com/LeadingWIB
twitter.com/ StrategySM
uk.linkedin.com/in/howtointerview
www.facebook.com/carole.fossey
www.instagram.com/carolefossey
www.carolefossey.com
www.leadingwomeninbiz.com
www.strategysocialmedia.com

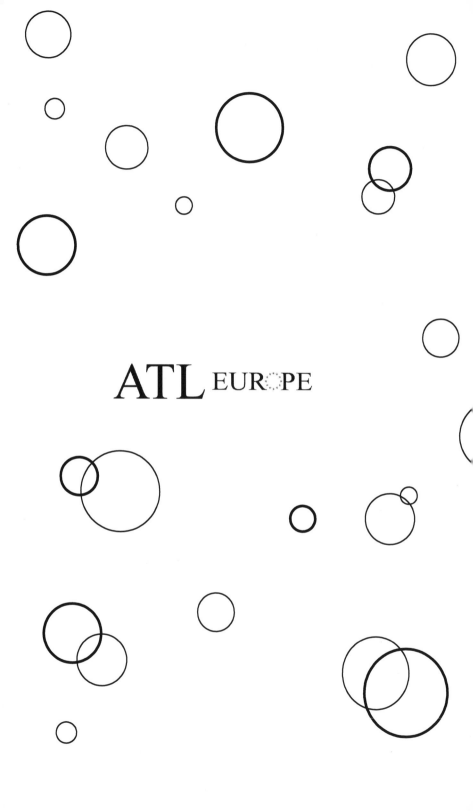

Chapter 16

TRANSFORMATION FROM THE OUTSIDE IN

Mindy Gibbins-Klein

You may have heard coaches talking about changing from the inside out, and it's true that any real change needs to happen inside you first before manifesting outwardly. However, sometimes things happen that absolutely rock your world, outside influences that affect you and your life. Things can happen that make you want to transform, or make you feel you *need* to. Although the outside event was the catalyst, it provides an opportunity for you to decide if you are going to use that impetus to change something about yourself or your life. That's why it's also important to be aware of what's happening *outside* of you, and see if you can use it in a positive way to create change *inside* you.

About four years ago, my husband and I experienced a big shock. Our son, 19 years old at the time, came out to us as transgender. It's not something we were expecting, as you may imagine. I don't think it is something any parent could expect to hear. This child, whom we had raised as our daughter, was telling us he was actually a boy. As parents, we didn't really understand it, and found it very difficult to get our heads around it and accept it.

I'm not proud of the way I acted at the time. I was not argumentative or openly hostile towards my son. In fact, we didn't discuss it at all. I tried to ignore it and brush it under the rug, hoping it would just go away. Of course, it did not go away and one day I had to take a long, hard look in the mirror and acknowledge that I was not being the person I knew I could be and should be. It was the beginning of my own important transformation into someone more loving and caring.

Life is always changing, so you always have another chance to transform yourself

We are always changing, whether we like it or not. As we get older, our skin sags, we may lose our hair, we sometimes get a little forgetful. Our circle of friends may change, and our outlook on life as well. And life is always changing around us too. Someone in your life will get sick, lose their job, end their marriage. The economy will go through its ups and downs. Politics will bring more change.

When something dramatic or traumatic happens in your life, it's another chance to choose whether to transform yourself or not. You know what, let's call it 'change', since 'transformation' can sound too big and scary when you are in a delicate, weakened or otherwise under-confident state.

There may be benefits in staying as you are. It's a familiar place. It requires little effort just to be swept along. At some point though, you may get a feeling that something has to change, and it may be time to face some hard truths about yourself. That is the defining moment, when you choose to create a big change in yourself.

How to consider and decide on your transformation

First, congratulate yourself for prioritising your personal development. Give yourself some space, give yourself a hug, give yourself some love. If you find even this hard to do, read the chapters on self-love in this book written by my colleagues.

Reflect quietly with a pen and paper. There are times when you just want to talk things through, but I have noticed that a lot of people instantly go to friends for 'advice' or post something online and gather many, many comments and opinions. The danger in doing that before you have thought things through for yourself is that you may be too easily influenced by people who happen to be very persuasive, especially when you are in a fragile state.

Take 20 minutes and sit quietly somewhere you don't normally go, with just pen and paper and no devices like phones or computers. Giving yourself space without technology reduces distractions, and the natural and kinaesthetic act of writing brings your right brain into the activity. You may have heard that's the side of the brain responsible for creativity and flow. You may not be in the habit of writing longhand, and that is exactly why you want to do it. It will bring a new experience and insights to you, through this simple act.

Ask yourself how you are feeling and write the answers down. Ask yourself what specifically is worrying or bothering you, and write that down too. Perhaps you want to make a list of pros and cons, advantages and disadvantages of the action you are considering taking. Ask the really hard questions and answer them.

After you have done your own thinking and reflection and have more clarity around the situation and options available to you, it may be time to share what is going on and get other ideas and advice.

Confide in the right people. It's funny, but in extreme situations, it's not always the obvious ones like close friends or family who will help you the most. In my case, I found someone I didn't know as well as other friends, but she was going through the same thing. And then I bumped into a friend I'd lost touch with, and she turned out to be the perfect person to listen to me practising my TEDx talk and give me sensitive feedback. It was actually easier speaking to people who didn't know me so well.

If you feel you need it, seek professional help, but make sure you work with the right people. Some coaches, counsellors, psychotherapists and other professionals have trained for many years. Others have just done a weekend course or an online course and then set themselves up in business. Be careful who you approach with your personal development goals and remember that even if you are paying for advice from a well-qualified professional, *you* have the final say and *you* can decide on the best course of action for you!

MINDY GIBBINS-KLEIN

Mindy Gibbins-Klein is the multi-award-winning founder of REAL Thought Leaders, The Book Midwife® and Panoma Press. She has presented to and coached over 50,000 leaders and entrepreneurs in 18 countries.

Mindy has authored and co-authored eight books, she has an enviable list of more than 700 published clients, many of whom have received excellent media coverage and book sales. Her TEDx talk, *Sometimes You Need to Change Yourself to Be Yourself,* which focuses on identity, self-esteem and transgender issues, has had nearly half a million views.

Her latest book, *The Thoughtful Leader,* challenges leaders to go beyond thought leadership and focus on consideration – of ideas and people.

www.mindygk.com
www.youtube.com/watch?v=B5W2AGg2nMo
twitter.com/MindyGK
twitter.com/bookmidwife
twitter.com/panomapress
www.facebook.com/mindy.gibbinsklein
www.youtube.com/bookmidwife
www.instagram.com/bookmidwife
www.linkedin.com/in/mindygibbinsklein

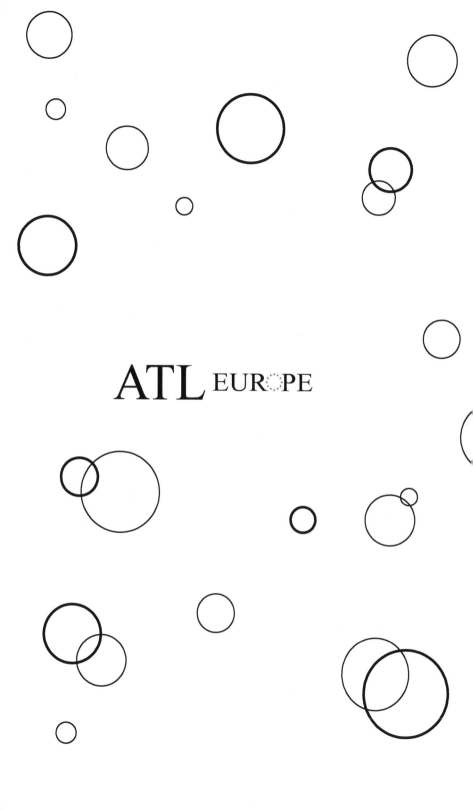

Chapter 17

THERE IS A RAINBOW IN EVERY THUNDERSTORM

Ania Jeffries

My train crash was the beginning of a wonderful, transformational chapter in my life. I can say this to you now but at that time I stopped dancing in the rain and entered a lonely period of darkness. I wore a mask for seven years, became invisible and lost the power of my voice. No one noticed. Neither did I. I always wore the biggest, most beautiful smile. My nickname was sunshine.

That day, 8 January 1991, was no different from any other. It was the year before the birth of our first child. Life was truly wonderful: recently married, living in a stunning leafy London suburb, PR manager for a telecommunications company, constantly being promoted and living *the* dream job. I was on a mission to create the life I had dreamt about for so many years and in an instance my life changed; it was put on hold.

I remember sitting on the train watching a father, trying to connect with his daughter and her being so rude to him that I wanted to stand up, to say: "Please stop humiliating him. Everyone can hear you. Say what you need to at home but don't behave like this so publicly." And then the train crashed. The conductor was high on cannabis. He drove into the buffers of Cannon Street station and I was in the carriage that concertinaed, where several innocent people died. There were hundreds of injuries.

The father disappeared under the crushed, coloured seats. You could see only his long legs. I will remember the daughter's piercing, powerful screams until I die. I can still hear them ringing loud and clear in my ears as if it were yesterday. Her shouting: "Daddy, I love you."

To this day, I have no idea whether he survived or not, but from that moment I have continued to question the power of communication, the impact of words on others. I constantly reflect on the fact that if he had died, she would never have been given the opportunity to apologise, to make things right again. That would be her last living memory of him.

So, what did I learn from this experience? Life is incredibly short. You all think you are living your best moments, but in truth you are probably surviving, living from day to day, not following your dreams nor inspiring everyone whose lives you touch. I learned that dealing with change can be painful, overwhelming, traumatic and very isolating. You can feel so alone. Somewhere, within you, you have to find your own strength, your own motivation to get your life back on track. No matter how fantastic your support network is, no matter how much you are loved, your closest and dearest cannot always help you.

You have to find the strength to help yourself and if you can't, *ask for help*. It's not a sign of weakness or failure. It's a sign of huge growth, transformation, strength. I cannot describe the feeling of overwhelm and fear I felt in that period after the crash.

I sued British Rail. It took seven years and I would never sue again. My winning will never replace the constant anxiety that came with dealing with the memories, the paperwork and the legal process, not only for me but also for my family. The letters dropping through the letterbox were a constant reminder that the nightmare was still not over. The trauma was constantly being played over and over in my mind like a film reel. The only way I could deal with this experience was to invest all my energy into my beautiful flower-kissed garden so that I did not have to deal with the pain and fear I felt deep inside.

My culture had taught me always to be strong. I wore a mask so that I would not have to disappoint anyone, show my pain. How wrong was I.

My tips for you

Life is a gift from the universe, so show deep gratitude for its beauty each and every day. In a breath, it can be taken away from you, can change you for the better or worse. The choice is yours. So, live every moment as if it was your last. Do not sweat the small stuff. Focus on what's important to you. Live your life with true purpose, passion, value not for anyone else, just for yourself.

Find the rainbow in your thunderstorm and turn your deep, darkest moments of adversity into moments of light, true sunshine. You *can*. You just have to adopt the right mindset, believe it and take action.

Being overwhelmed, experiencing fear and change are part of your daily life challenges. Create the right positive mindset to help you deal with these moments and always ask for help. Never go it alone and never ever give up. You may think you are weak, but your weakness is in fact a sign of huge strength, an inspiration to others. Showing your vulnerability takes huge courage.

Share your story. It will help others. You never know what others are dealing with in their own lives. The moment you share your story is the moment your journey of true transformation begins; a new chapter of recovery and growth is awakened not just for yourself but for others too.

Always look forward. Never backward. And never blame others. It doesn't serve you. Only holds you back from being the brightest star in the sky.

Question the words you use with others. Your message may come from the right place with the best intention, but unless delivered in the right love language, it may be painful and can take others a long time to heal. So be mindful of the words you use.

And above all, know that if you don't believe in you, I do. Know that I believe in you. My purpose is to help you shine your light on this world, to help you use your voice with confidence to create a life of happiness, passion and value.

ANIA JEFFRIES

Ania Jeffries is an award-winning coach, the founder of Women Work, an international best-selling author of *The Pay it Forward Series: Notes to My Younger Self*, a licensed neurolinguistic programming (NLP) practitioner, progression mentor for The Prince's Trust, event organiser and radio broadcaster for *UK Health Radio*. Her next book, *Gain Confidence in 24 Hours, The Toolkit to Help You Grow* will be released in autumn 2018.

Ania's vision is to build a global revolution of confident entrepreneurs who speak with powerful voices. She specialises in personal growth, confidence, empowerment and self-improvement.

A mother of three and wife, she is totally dedicated to providing 10 million men and women with transformational, empowering media, coaching tools and strategies to use the power of their authentic voice with confidence, to unleash their full potential.

www.nextstepmentor.com
www.facebook.com/ania.jeffries
FB Nextstepmentor123
Twitter: @JeffriesAnia
Instagram: @nextstepmentor123

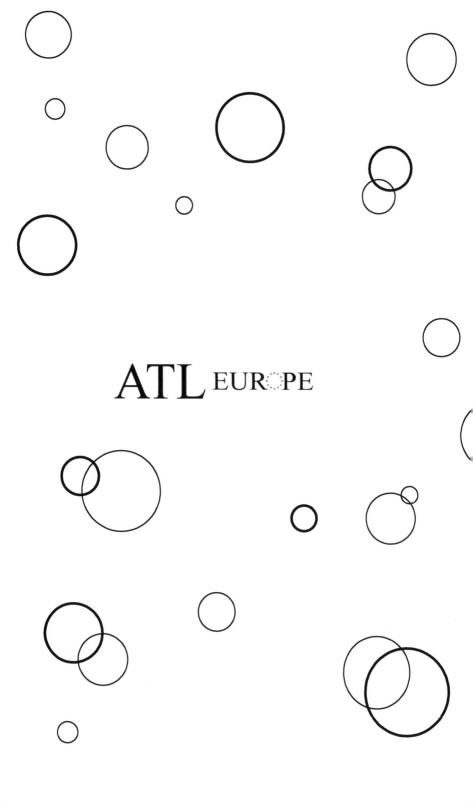

ATL EUR●PE

Chapter 18

PAY ATTENTION

Garry Jones

You are familiar with the story of building on sand are you not? You of course understand that a *strong* foundation is everything.

Sensible is it not to be on solid ground? If I said, "Can you *now* recall a time that you felt you were not on solid ground? A time where you needed more understanding, knowledge or *experience*." Of course, you just have. If I shared a few techniques for you to help prevent that in the future, would you *benefit*? Of course.

Mind, body and spirit. Each of us is on our own journey. What I am advocating here, is to get your foundations solid. In other words, the body, chemicals and electrical circuits within you. You may find it helps with the mind and spirit exercises you undertake. Check it.

That with a solid foundation the other tasks are easier. Here, my words will focus on the body, to open the doors to mind and spirit.

What I am going to share is concise and to the point. I do not have the space here to share all the science and background. Do your own research and analysis if you will. As one of my mentors said: "Be careful of too much 'analyse', it ends in anal lies!" However, as you can tell I do like to do my own research, if you wish to know more check out my YouTube postings or use search engines.

I have one fundamental value set I follow, and I will share that with you *now*. I believe it is healthy to challenge what is put before us. The ABC:

A   Accept nothing

B   Believe nothing

C   Check everything

Which is what I am asking you to *do* with these techniques. The real test is the '*check everything*' part. It is very easy to do the first two using a solid set of *beliefs* or truths that *are yours*. The most important part is to check it. *Do* the *exercises*, and from there you can qualify their effectiveness and relevance to you *now*. We could move into quantum physics and the role of observers affecting the experiment, which I would love to do as that subject fascinates me, but…

Pay attention technique 1: Thoughts

Trust me, this will reward you massively. While you read the previous pages of this book, I am sure that your internal dialogue ran wild. Many voices chattering away inside your head. This does not mean you are mentally ill. Some of us experience our own voice; others have many voices. You do it a little differently. The internal talking gets in the way of you truly reading or listening. Your sensory acuity is impaired by the clutter in your head. Some people do this in a peculiar way; I am one of them. When concentrating, I poke my tongue out – although I quickly learned to avoid this action in martial arts. This simple exercise will hold two of your sensory inputs in check.

In the English language, there is a saying: "Hold your tongue" and it is, like most linguistics, a literal fact. Your tongue moves inside your mouth as you internally talk. It uses vast amounts of brainpower with the sensors on the tongue and connection to the language sections of your brain.

This is thinking. Your tongue moves inside your mouth when you are thinking. You are not listening when you are thinking. Take control of your tongue!

When reading or listening, imagine a small ball of olive oil behind your teeth. Keep it there by pushing your tongue against it. Push too hard and it will burst; fail to push enough and it will also burst.

Keep it steady, relax your throat and jaw a little. Let all the muscles soften and relax. You are now able to see and hear much more. Information is absorbed in a far more efficient way. It feels comfortable, and you will remember details and facts more readily. You will not feel the urge to interject while communicating or run off at a tangent when reading. Notice how the dialogue reduced, and the chatter inside your head almost disappeared.

This is a fantastic technique, and I recommend not only using it to read the rest of this and any other book: I highly recommend you use it in all your communications. It will help you still your mind and choose your thoughts more wisely.

Pay attention technique 2: Emotions

There are a number of drugs your body produces that enable you to *feel good*. Serotonin is one of them. (You can find a description of others on my website.) A common complaint associated with mobile phones is the narcissism of selfies. A common experience for you and me, at times, is depression. The *act* of not feeling *good* about yourself.

In a moment, I will share with you a simple exercise related to a contributory factor involved. When you look towards the floor you reduce your serotonin production (a neurotransmitter that is triggered by the pineal gland in the brain and secreted in the gut). When it is secreted, it contributes to you feeling good. You know, when we say: "Gut feelings". So, when you are on your phone, looking down, you are not feeling so good. Conversely, when you *look up* (particularly to the right-hand side) you produce serotonin. You know, when you are taking selfies, for instance. Addicted to selfies or just feeling good?

Look up. Do it often. When you awake. Before you *open your eyes*. Throughout the day. Go outside and look up to the skies. At night go look at the stars or the Moon. Even better if you *stand* up *straight* or *sit* with a *straight* spine. *Smile*. How *simple* is that to do, and the *reward* is to *feel good*. Awesome.

"Remember to look up at the stars and not down at your feet."

Professor Stephen Hawking

Pay attention technique 3: Body

A common excuse I hear from clients is they do not have time to *exercise*. Is that something you might say to yourself? *Now*, perhaps you do not have time, not to. Exercise that is. I wonder. So here is something that will only take four minutes. We can all find *four minutes* to spare, for the good of our health. (I do suggest you get a health check first before engaging in high-intensity training.)

Download an app for Tabata. Or you can time or count the seconds.

Perform any exercise as *fast* as you can for 20 seconds and *then rest* for 10. Repeat it for eight sets or times. (Check out my YouTube channel.)

That easy. Try it. Decide upon exercises that will suit your age, fitness levels etc. Listen to your body. Particularly pain. Pain is the body saying it needs attention. Pay attention!

Check the benefits from your research or learn to experience them for yourself. The experience option works better for me. A traveller spent 30 years wandering across Asia searching for the one true guru who could tell her how to achieve enlightenment. Finally, she believed she had found the one. In a cave deep in the mountains, having gained audience, she the one true guru agreed to share the three methods which I share with you now:

"Pay attention … pay attention … pay attention"

Pay attention to your thoughts.

Pay attention to your emotions.

Pay attention to your body.

They hold some of the keys to your enlightenment.

(There was a not-so-hidden code in this chapter. Did you pay attention to discover it?)

GARRY JONES

Garry Jones is a global linguistics leader, international speaker, martial arts instructor and transformational coach. He has experienced 20 years in the corporate world and to date 15 years with his own businesses, which gives him a complete understanding of businesses large and small, and the people who work in them.

From the age of seven, Garry has been involved with martial arts and alongside his successful coaching career, he owns and runs a Muay Thai boxing gym. His vision is to have a positive impact upon 300 million people or more by using the many techniques in which he has been trained, by the very best qualified in the world.

He lives with his family in the UK, in the countryside, working with clients nationally and internationally. He also spends time doing charity work for those with mental health challenges.

www.GarryJonesCoaching.com/
www.facebook.com/garry.jones.94695
b-m.facebook.com/garryjonescoaching27
uk.linkedin.com/in/garry-jones-coaching
twitter.com/GarryNLPCoach
www.instagram.com/garryjonescoaching/?hl=en
www.youtube.com/channel/UC5S9wejaYlpVWdN6jFKoi0Q

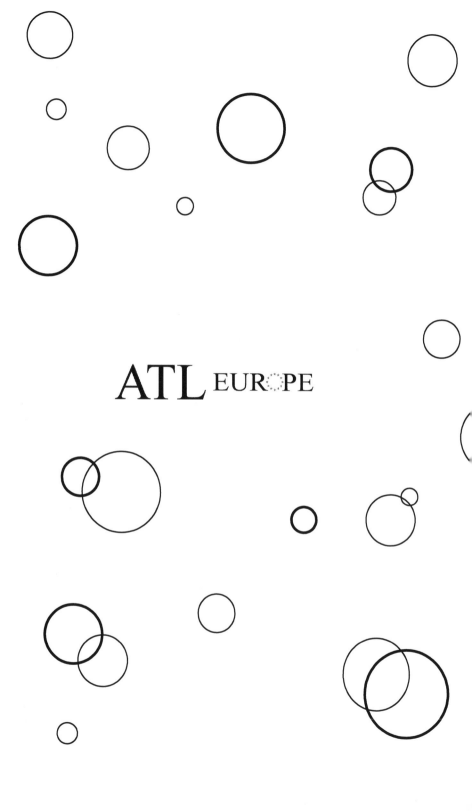

Chapter 19

YOU MATTER

Liz Keaney

The journey

My transformational journey started on the fateful or blessed day (depending on your perspective) 11 years ago, the day the second cancer diagnosis was confirmed. I couldn't believe this was happening to me again. It was only six months since I'd recovered from a major operation and some particularly unpleasant and invasive treatment… and now this.

In my shocked state, I was only half-listening to the words from the medic. Then it happened. I recall distinctively that everything became still and I heard a voice. I knew the voice well – it was my own, speaking silently in my head. The message was clear: "Find some answers."

I had no idea where to start but found myself at the local library locating books on health and specifically nutrition. Reading felt hugely empowering: the more I learned about how I could help myself, the less I felt like a victim, if you will. The scientific jigsaw of how an inappropriate diet and lifestyle exacerbates stress and increases vulnerability to illness started to make sense to me. Alarmingly, it became very evident that with my demanding corporate job and lifestyle I was perpetuating my own stress. It was time to embark on some serious self-kindness.

Fast-forward a few weeks. Once again, I was browsing for more books on nutrition and to this day I don't know why I turned and reached impulsively for a book leaning out of the shelf to my right. As I did so, I looked up and noticed with horror that the sign above this shelf was labelled 'self-help' in big, bold letters.

Self-help

OMG, this was embarrassing, almost shameful. Here I was, suited and booted, en route to a corporate appointment. In my mind, I didn't fit the profile of someone flaky, hippy or 'woo woo'. I was most definitely not the sort of person that would have publicly acknowledged that I needed help.

However, I must admit this book was the catalyst for changing my life. *Why?* Because this book gave me a new level of awareness – consciousness. This encouraged me to focus on what health I did have, not the other way around. It invited me to have gratitude for my physical body and all the things I could do. I learned to see my body as a place of nurture that I could feed kindly, not only with food, but also with kind thoughts, words and intentions.

From there I was introduced a new reality, one where I saw my body as more than a collection of its parts: an energetic field that was within me and radiated from me. My eyes were opened to the possibility that there could be a connection between my physical body and my emotions and that my mind was in my heart, not in my head.

Turning a light on

"When the student is ready, the teacher appears."

It was a bit like turning a light on. I started seeking similar books, ones that explained the mind, body and soul connections, mind mastery and energy awareness. Gosh, I surprised myself. I loved this self-help stuff and whenever I got the opportunity, I'd be back searching for books that could inspire me even more.

Something within me acknowledged that I could be a master of all aspects of my life as well as my wellness. The more I read, the more answers I found. That was 11 years ago.

I left the corporate job and today I enjoy a fabulous new perspective on life and possess health, happiness and wealth. I feel compelled to pass on everything I know about self-nurture, self-worth and self-connection as well as what I've learned about the link between science, senses and our soul.

"To be teachable we need to know what it is we are seeking."

You matter

The essence of the transformational lesson I'd like to share with you is that *you matter*. The interpretation of your life has a direct correlation with the level of self-kindness you afford yourself. Through self-kindness, you can connect to your inner magnificence. Through this magnificence you can be the co-creator of your life.

Your magnificence is the make-up of your words, inner talk and thoughts which all have energy. Develop a consciousness of words you use, your inner talk and thoughts as they act like a mirror affecting the subtle vibration you present to the world. In the same way, examine the beliefs you hold. It's entirely possible they are inherited, outdated and no longer serve you. Understand the power of your subconscious mind and how it is the real co-creator of your life. Get absolute clarity on what you do want in your life and why. Put your focus here with real intention, rather than noticing what is lacking in your life or what you don't want. Play a mind movie of your ideal life often – give it vibrancy and most of all give it emotion. Feel the feeling of the wish fulfilled.

What you put into your physical body

Develop a consciousness of foods that nurture and nourish you, rather than foods that simply fuel you. Respect your body and thank it often for all the work it does for you. Understand that your physical body is a reflection of your emotional body. Express, don't suppress, your feelings. If it feels inappropriate to express your feelings verbally, then journal your feelings or use visualisation release techniques.

The extent to which you connect with Mother Earth and God or the universe

Use any opportunity to connect with nature, ground your energy and be still with all that is. In the stillness, you can connect to your truth – your authentic, intuitive spiritual self. Become your own student; the listener and observer of your life. Learn from your own experiences especially the ones that challenge you.

No one can diminish your magnificence unless you allow them. Keep your magnificence dial turned up high and watch serendipity happen: beautiful people and events will magnetise into your life. Namaste.

LIZ KEANEY

Liz Keaney (known as the KindnessCODE™ Warrior) is an inspirational speaker, author, transformational coach and mentor for The Girls' Network, empowering you to become the magnificent co-creator of your life.

Her original career in financial services spanned almost 30 years, until two serious health diagnoses put life on a different track. This blessing in disguise forced Liz to look more closely at her life and in doing so she unlocked something she refers to as the KindnessCODE™.

She left her corporate job to become a self-kindness advocate, gaining expertise in naturopathic nutrition, mindfulness, EFT, matrix reimprinting, energy healing, law of attraction and qigong.

Liz coaches clients from all cultures, nationalities and backgrounds and through her workshops and retreats in the UK and internationally she helps people realise the potentiality of their lives.

Her book, *Warrior Women: How to be Magnificent through the Courage of Self Kindness,* is available at www.amazon.co.uk

www.lizkeaney.com
www.facebook.com/Kindnesscode/
twitter.com/lizkeaney
www.instagram.com/lizkeaney

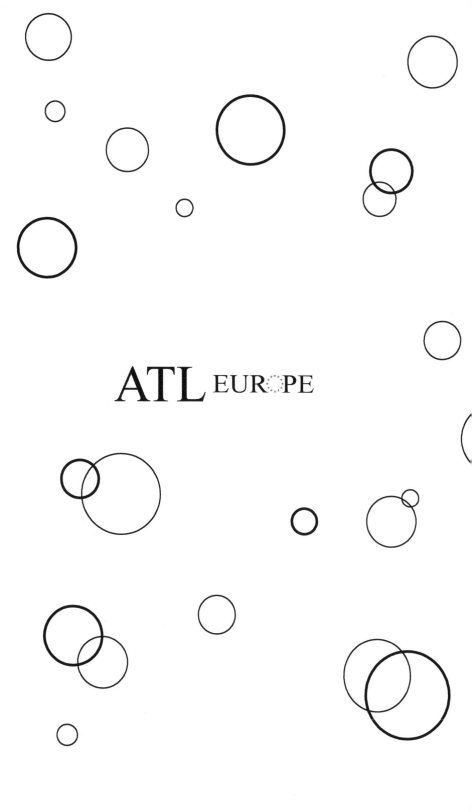

Chapter 20

HOW TO BE HAPPY

Caroline Laschkolnig

We live our lives in a loop. Do this. Do that. Go home. Relax. Repeat.

Yet, I feel, most people get no satisfaction of this daily routine: they live on, day by day, feeling constantly that something's wrong, imperfect. For most people, the likely answer to the question: "How can you be happy?" would be: "More income, more friends, less stress."

What if I told you that it could be so much easier? That you can be happy now. Happiness is seen as a luxury, something you have to work for, strive for and perhaps then you will be rewarded only with a shred of joy. But I think that this belief is utter nonsense. Still, it is deeply implanted in people's brains. I cannot make you believe me, but maybe you could consider this: happiness isn't a lifestyle, or a luxury. No, it's a choice. And this choice is yours to make.

Of course, sometimes it can be hard to choose happiness over anything else, but I have a few tricks for that.

Step 1: The choice

Right now, as you are reading this, you can simply choose to be happy. Read it out loud: "I choose to be happy." You can decide on this feeling right now over any other emotion. Instead of being uncomfortable because of the way you're sitting, worrying about your sick sibling or what others are thinking about you, feeling bad about the pressure parents or your boss give you regarding your performance, etc., you can choose to be happy. Refocus. Right now. Smile!

Step 2: Appreciation

Appreciation is a major help whenever you have a hard time making the choice to be happy. Whether you appreciate the greenness of the leaves on the way to your job or school every day, or that you succeeded in doing something you have been working on for ages, or anything you can feel remotely good about (but not at another person's cost), however small, try to genuinely feel good about that.

If you have trouble finding anything to appreciate in your immediate surroundings, compare yourself with the average person 100 years ago. The worse you feel, the more centuries you should travel back mentally. You'll quickly see that the past wasn't always better. Did the average knight have a tap in their own kitchen with a supply of clean water? Did they even have a kitchen? No, they lived in cold castles, had to wear armour half their weight and died, if lucky, age 40, with hardly any teeth left. So, I guess we don't live that badly, do we?

Step 3: Passion for self-compassion

I know it's not always easy to feel good, especially when something happens and impacts you in a negative way. If I feel down and I know I could feel better, and I truly want to but still find no way to cheer myself up, I remember my passions and as soon as possible,

I make time for some craftwork, painting or spending time with my dog.

Write down your top three favourite activities that make it feel as though time is standing still.

1._____

2._____

3._____

Whether this activity is dancing, painting, working out or meeting up with friends, when you feel lost in this large world, cut yourself off from all media – turn off your phone and TV, close your laptop, mute the radio and lose yourself in one of your passions.

Step 4: Unleash the hero in you

Everyone has problems. Usually they are all relatively small and insignificant, yet everyone is convinced that their problem is of utmost priority.

A thing that may seem obvious is that when you don't have a problem, you don't have to worry. If, however, you do have a problem and you can do something about it or influence the solution, and you have done everything in your power to do so, you can stop worrying, because (hopefully) you have done all you could and have no further influence on the outcome.

Doing everything in your power and using all possibilities is not always easy. Why are all the known heroes brave and courageous? Because if you don't have courage, you might not be ready to face all available options to solve your problem. So, be brave!

If you can't do anything about your problem at all, then there is no need to worry either. I usually think about the relevance of a particular problem from the perspective of six months' time, a year's time and five years' time and usually I can see that it actually won't matter much if I happen to mess it up now.

Step 5: Allow all emotions but choose happiness

Being happy doesn't mean jumping around and clapping your hands 24/7, as things happen in life and it's OK to feel every other emotion than happiness. However, be fully aware that you are sad or angry or frustrated. By all means, experience this feeling to the fullest and as soon as you have had enough of it, feel happy again.

Appreciate the little things in life and feel genuine joy. If you feel like crap, arrange time for yourself to live your passions and you will feel better again. Don't worry and consciously choose to be happy.

CAROLINE LASCHKOLNIG

Caroline Laschkolnig, born in Austria in 2004, is a co-founder of ATL Junior, a young leader, a deep thinker and an empath. Naturally spiritual, she has meditated since childhood. Since the age of 10, she has been involved in social and environmental projects: an 'Orangutan Project', to raise awareness of them losing their natural habitat, and 'No Blood On My Clothes', to make a real improvement in the life of women sewing clothes for the big fashion companies.

Caroline is a true Renaissance girl: raised trilingual, she speaks English, German, Polish and French, and is excited about starting to learn Spanish soon.

Her passions are crafting, painting, writing, reading, acting, dancing, leading deep conversations with scientists and artists about interesting issues not tackled at school.

She has danced ballet for eight years and performed in *The Nutcracker* with the Russian National Ballet.

Caroline became a national champion at K2 kayaking, but has chosen to focus on her artistic and scientific passions.

Caroline.Laschkolnig@MonikaLaschkolnig.com

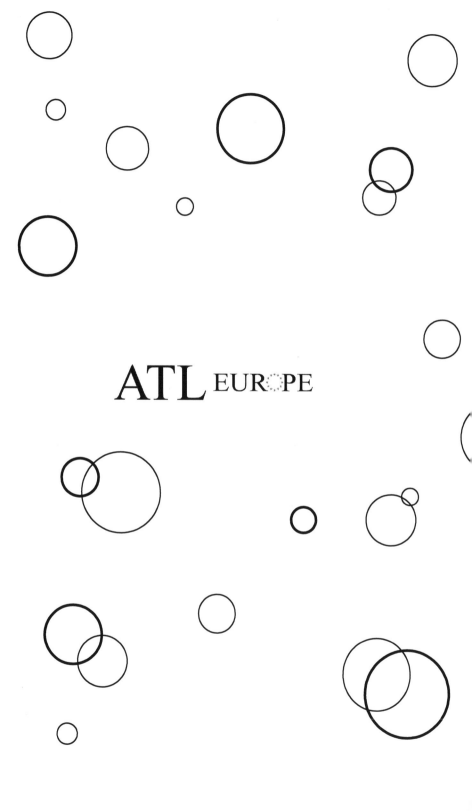

Chapter 21

LIFE IS HAPPENING FOR YOU, NOT AGAINST YOU

Martin Laschkolnig

"Surrender!" says life.

"Oh no," says the ego, "look, I've got it all under control."

"Do you?" asks life.

"Of course!" replies the ego proudly.

"All right then," says life and takes its course…

"Phew, well, that was not how I had it planned," groans the ego.

And so it all starts from the beginning.

Does that sound familiar? Or do you regularly plan on having a crisis? Well of course not. But let me ask you in another way: the last time you tried to control life, how well did it work out?

I have asked this question of many people in my talks and consultation visits. And you know what? Each and every one had to smile – some rather cheekily, others more embarrassedly – but not one said, "Of course, it worked out brilliantly!"

So, we all know, when the rubber hits the road, life is taking its course, whether it's to our liking or not. I have tried to control life, for many, many years. I've done it all – to-do lists, planning, goal setting, visualisation, willpower and massive action. And it all worked. Well, sometimes… and sometimes not so much.

And I came to realise that there is a limited scope of things that we can achieve when we operate from ego. I have come to the conviction that each and every one of us has a purpose for being on this planet. And as long as we are following that calling, we are in alignment. Then life works out.

If we are not, life has its ways to let us know we are off track. We get depressed, have this nagging feeling of dissatisfaction, feel stuck or in the wrong place. And if we don't listen to that, a crisis is life's way to tell us that we are seriously off track. I experienced this several times in my life and it took me a while to figure it all out. At first I ignored it, pushed harder, worked more. But life isn't the one to give up easily either, so it gave me another hint. A stronger one. But I was still too daft to get it. Don't get me wrong, I was doing a lot of personal development work and yet I was ignoring that I was actually working against what life wanted for me, because it seemed so big, so daunting.

But note this – life is happening for us and not against us, so even the challenges and crises that we are facing at times are holding a gift. In my case, I just didn't see it.

So finally, life presented me with a crisis so big that I could not see a way out anymore. I had only one thing left to do – to surrender. As all other options were exhausted, I let go and let life take over.

But to my surprise, when I let life – this loving, higher intelligence, that we are all connected to – take the reins, something interesting happened. It took care of me. Not quite the way I expected, but with a simplicity, an elegance, a grace that was close to miraculous.

There is no question whether life will be taking you along, only by when you will go voluntarily. When you finally start trusting the flow of life, it will carry you as it did with me.

In my case it took me from a state of deep, deep crisis to a state of inner peace and love – in a matter of just a couple of months. Just like that? No, it wasn't that simple. It was quite demanding, and I played along. As if I had had any other chance anyway… and suddenly, sometimes seemingly out of nowhere, people, methods and circumstances showed up to guide me step by step into my most profound personal transformation yet.

What was my contribution? I went with the process, did not resist it, as scary as that was at times. I faced my shadows and did my best to let go, forgive myself and all others around me and let life take the lead. Finally, I paid attention to the signs that presented themselves and followed the path that life laid out for me.

So, am I enlightened now? No, I still have my human moments, of course. Quite a few actually, obviously. But I can say that the periods of acceptance and peace in my life get longer and longer every month that I keep on trusting that life is guiding me.

Actually, it was hugely relaxing to realise that I am not the one running the show here. Because this means that we are not responsible for the outcome any longer. Our responsibility lies with this very moment, lies in what you are doing now. Are you showing up fully and contributing your best for the greater good of all? That's perfect. That's enough. And actually, that's all that you have control over anyway.

What can you do practically to tune into the flow of life? Here are three practical things that I found helpful on my path.

1. Practise moments of gratitude

As often as possible, find things to be grateful for. Simple things, like turning on the electric light, or making a video call on your smartphone. Or when you see a beautiful cloud in the sky, or a loving gesture between a parent and a kid on the street. Random things – there is so much to be appreciative of and grateful for.

Notice them and let this warm feeling of love and gratitude spread in your body.

2. Ask and watch for signs

I have started to offer my ignorance to life. What do I mean by that? Whenever I am faced with a situation that I don't have an answer for right now I think by myself: "Thank you, life, for showing me the answer to this one, for giving me the clarity, and so forth." And rest in this feeling of gratitude again that life has the capability to show you an answer. Because of course it has: that is not the question. The question is whether you are ready to let it in, and that is something that you definitely have under control.

3. Don't believe everything that you think

"Don't believe everything that you think" is a sentence I learned from Byron Katie, the founder of a process called 'The Work', that has influenced me a lot. We all have this instance in our mind that I like to call 'monkey mind'. Monkey mind is fantastic at building scenarios, worrying, judging and criticising. Don't let it be the master, but use it when critical thinking is necessary. The only caveat is that it is way less necessary than we were conditioned to believe. I regularly send mine off into the corner, saying: "No, we don't have to figure that out now. Shut up and thank you, life, for showing me what to do next."

4. Let go of your suppressed emotions and disappointments

This is actually a bonus point – I am a big believer in letting go of old resentments, hurts and rejections. Go to my website and you'll find a few processes for doing that easily and effortlessly.

So, trust life. Get real. Expect miracles. Have fun along the ride.

MARTIN LASCHKOLNIG

Martin Laschkolnig is connecting the worlds of spirituality and business. He is an international keynote speaker, trainer, coach and entrepreneur. He served as the President of the German Speakers Association from 2015–17 and has inspired audiences from San Diego to Cape Town and throughout Europe.

He is an expert in motivation, self-esteem, confidence and inner peace and how these affect leaders, their teams and the performance of people and enterprises.

Combining an economic education and entrepreneurial background with studies in Buddhist philosophy and theory of perception with Tibetan monk scholars in India, led to a different approach to view and solve our problems.

Martin's latest programme is called 'Trusting the Flow of Life', which shows a practical and simple approach to stop resisting with letting go of drama and stress and moving into inner peace. He teaches a simple process that can be easily integrated in everyone's daily life.

www.MartinLaschkolnig.at
www.facebook.com/laschkolnig
www.instagram.com/martinlaschkolnig
www.linkedin.com/in/laschkolnig/

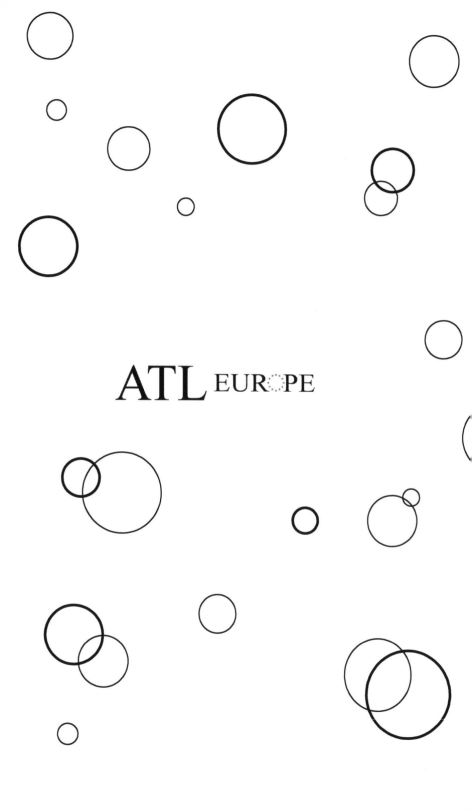

ATL EUROPE

Chapter 22

THROUGH SELF-FORGIVENESS TO SELF-LOVE AND HAPPINESS

Monika Laschkolnig

Self-love, self-acceptance, self-worth and self-care start with self-forgiveness as the first step. When you hold grudges and resentments towards yourself, you don't allow yourself to experience happiness or step into your greatness. As your own worst critic, you are not able to accept yourself the way you are and tend to put constant demands on yourself.

As long as you do not forgive yourself for the past mistakes and failures, you hinder yourself from loving yourself fully and do not offer yourself enough self-care that you would need to feel really good. Even though your innate sense of self-worth tells you that you are lovable and good enough, if you don't forgive yourself for some past actions or reactions, you hold the bar too low as a form of a subconscious self-punishment and accept life experiences that do not express self-love.

All forgiveness boils down to self-forgiveness, even in a situation where you perceive past events as hurt, violence, injustice and abuse consciously inflicted on you by another. Things happened. That is a fact. But what is it that makes you feel hurt, let down, abandoned or unworthy?

In the first place, you have projected your expectations on to someone, for example, your parents, children, teachers, friends, believing they would behave differently, and you feel disappointed that they didn't. Most of them were, most probably, not even aware of all your thoughts, wishes and needs. Then you judged whether their actions met your expectations. If they did not, you felt hurt and disappointed.

So who made you hurt? In most cases you yourself. I am not referring to physical pain inflicted on you but the emotional pain in a form of a sense of injustice, unworthiness, being mistreated, unwanted, ignored, neglected or abandoned. They all result in resentment, shame or guilt, which you tend to carry for a long time. All that hinders you from being joyful, happy, fulfilled and fully successful.

Had your parents promised you before you were born to love you unconditionally and please you in the way you wished to be treated? Or were you possibly born to a couple of, in some way, broken or emotionally hurt humans who only did the best they could?

Did your friends promise to you to be perfect? Did your teachers assure you they were balanced and unmistaken? None of them did. I do not excuse their actions, I am only drawing your attention to the fact that you expected something of them that they were not able to deliver. In your eyes, they failed or betrayed you by not acting as a loving parent, grateful child, good friend or able teacher, for example, which caused you pain.

Self-forgiveness starts when you take a look at the past events from a different angle. I was struggling for years with forgiving several events from my childhood, until I finally realised that I had projected expectations on myself and others, which none of us had been able to fulfil. We might wish to interact only with the best side of others, but we deal with imperfect humans.

I realised that I had let some events describe me, which caused me to feel bad about myself. I suddenly could see situations from my and others' life as pictures in front of my eyes and I captured the realisation in the poem-prayer, *I Forgive Myself*, which I would like to share with you here. I read it every day for 30 days, letting the new understanding and an ability to forgive myself sink into my system fully.

It's a very simple, yet powerful method. Start with acknowledging the pain resulting from what had happened and tell yourself: "I'm sorry you had to experience that." Allow this sense of self-compassion to fill you up.

Then move into seeing past events from a new angle, which will grant you with inner peace, a sense of freedom, security, feeling worthy and lovable:

I Forgive Myself

I forgive myself
For having made all the mistakes
Had I known better, I would have chosen differently
So I forgive myself

I forgive myself
For having felt hurt when I didn't feel loved and wanted
They never promised me they would, so it was just my unmet
expectation
So I forgive myself

I forgive myself
For believing them when they said I'm unworthy
They didn't see my light and spoke out of their shadows
So I forgive myself

I forgive myself
For feeling scared and getting hurt when they acted out of anger
I know now it was not about me – it was their inability to cope with life
better
So I forgive myself

I forgive myself
For the suffering when I felt I didn't belong
It made me journey inwards and find my spirit, my true home
So I forgive myself

I forgive myself
For feeling let down
They did what they believed was OK – my hurt came from what I wanted
from them
So I forgive myself

I forgive myself
For having believed that my love was worthless
My love is precious – but they were too hurt to open up to it
So I forgive myself

I forgive myself
For having learnt not to love myself
I accepted it was right not to care about myself, but now I know who I am
So I forgive myself

I forgive myself
For taking things as directed against me
They were just events that took place because the doers were not happy with
their life
So I forgive myself

I forgive myself
For having given my power away, letting them decide for me
I felt fear or didn't know better, but now I'm ready to learn
So I forgive myself

I forgive myself
For having expressed hurtful judgments of myself, which made me judge others
too
I've finally tasted the sweetness of love over the bitterness of the
critique-poison
So I forgive myself

I forgive myself
For believing I'm unable, I'm small, I don't count
I allow myself to acknowledge the truth that I have gifts and I'm worthy
So I forgive myself

I forgive myself
That it took me so long to learn to forgive
But I was willing to learn
So now I forgive and start to respect myself

MONIKA LASCHKOLNIG

Monika Ewa Laschkolnig is quite an exceptional blend: an expert on inner transformation, bestselling author, an intuitive guide and a spiritual teacher. She has 20 years' entrepreneurial experience and has engaged in deep spiritual practice since she was 13.

Having trained in the West and the Far East, Monika is a modern mystic without a monastery, standing in the midst of life's business, making a difference in people's lives through her educational business on one hand and, on the other, through her seminars, programmes, books and philanthropic activities, while continuing with her own inner work.

One of Monika's greatest passions is guiding people to a lasting transformation in workshops on modern spirituality, self-love and self-forgiveness, intuition, conscious parenting, self-worth, and accessing your inner wisdom. She is an interfaith ordained ministerial counsellor, focused on the universal truth and what connects us all beyond rituals, terminology and cultural differences. She combines practical entrepreneurial skills with leading an awakened life and being a conscious parent.

www.MonikaLaschkolnig.com
www.facebook.com/MonikaLaschkolnigAuthor/
www.linkedin.com/in/monikalaschkolnig
www.twitter.com/MonikaAuthor
www.instagram.com/monikalaschkolnig

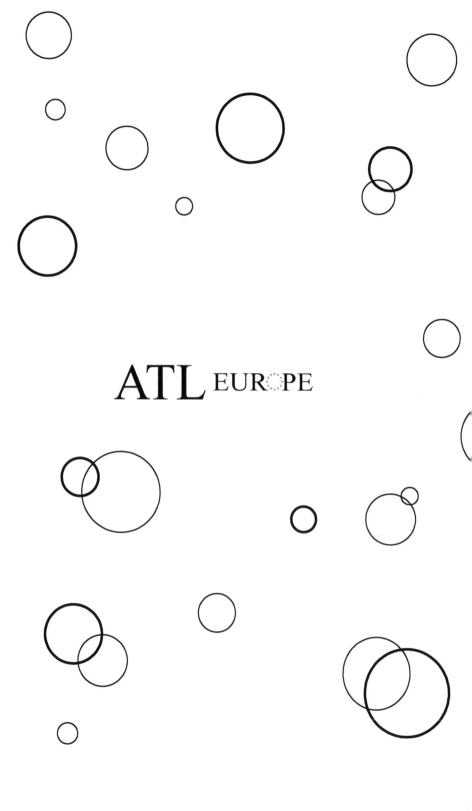

Chapter 23

CONSCIOUSNESS@WORK: "AS WITHIN, SO WITHOUT"... A TRANSFORMATIONAL JOURNEY TO FULFILMENT

Malou Laureys

Focusing on being fulfilled rather than being successful

I've encountered a lot of people who were 'successful' according to the norms of family, society or culture. Yet, deep inside they felt empty or restless. They were asking themselves: "Is this it? Is this life?"

I was one of them. After studying civil engineering and getting an MBA, at the age of 26, I became the managing director of a small company. I had created a life that I thought would lead me to happiness: I had a partner, a nice job title, an expensive car, a villa in a good neighbourhood, lots of friends, and exotic holidays. On a deeper level I felt empty, and unconsciously tried to fill this emptiness with binge eating, shopping, TV, a busy social life, a full calendar and setting even bigger goals in life.

Now, in my coaching and therapy practice, I see more and more 'successful' women and men feeling empty or restless inside. They have what a lot of people dream of. What they don't have is fulfilment.

Why does being successful not automatically lead to being fulfilled? Both have in common 'the achievement of something desired'. The goals you set to become 'successful' are more often than not dictated by your ego, influenced by your past experiences, upbringing, family, culture.

But reaching 'fulfilment' is about the achievement of your heart or soul's desire, meaning you do something that meets the purpose of your life, that fulfils the reason for your incarnation, that life wants you to do, that gives you inner joy. Fulfilling your soul's desire coincides with doing something that you love, you are good at, the world needs, and brings you abundance (whatever abundance means for your soul). Thus, fulfilment will lead to success, while success will not necessarily lead to fulfilment.

Connecting to your essence to listen to your soul's desire

But how do you know what life wants for you? How do you co-create with life your soul's mission, which will lead you to fulfilment and inner joy? You need to have a deep connection with your inner core or essence to hear and create your calling. But your essence is often buried under multiple layers of protective patterns, beliefs and behaviours that you developed since childhood to get the love and acceptance of your caretakers.

These patterns are primary parts of you that protect your wounded parts and push away undesirable parts that threatened your survival and have become disowned. Bringing all these primary parts, wounded parts and disowned parts to light, accepting and transforming them, will help you to be more in touch with your spontaneous creative self and core being. The more these layers become transparent, the more you will be authentic and free, the more you will hear the voice of your inner guidance helping you to fulfil your soul's mission.

An effective way to become aware of your primary parts, wounded parts and disowned parts is to look at what you attract in your outside world, and how you react to it. How you experience your outside world is a mirror of your inside world, of your conscious and unconscious beliefs, of what you hold on to from your past. *As within, so without.*

A primary part that I find present in a lot of my 'successful, yet not fulfilled' clients, is the 'pusher'. This is a part in you that always finds something more to do, that creates a never-ending to-do list, that makes you feel guilty if you take a 10-minute rest. It is a very driven, forceful and active part. If this part is dominating the scene in your inner psyche, the opposite 'easy going' part, which allows you to relax, is disowned (not accepted or underdeveloped) and this blocks you from being in contact with your soul's longing.

To feel the subtle voice of your calling, this part has to be balanced with a more surrendering part that allows you to rest and relax, to be in nature, to be playful, to just 'be' rather than 'do'. You can become aware of this overactive pusher in you if you find that in your outside world you are judgmental toward or strongly reactive to people that you judge as 'lazy' or if you notice yourself being irritated by co-workers, friends, family members not 'doing' enough. With a balance between your 'doing' and 'being' part, you wouldn't attract conflicting situations regarding this theme, or you wouldn't have a strong reaction to it.

Using (your reaction to) your outside world as a mirror for your inside world

For most conflicts or stressful situations that you are facing with people from your outer world, you can find inside your inner world at least one imbalance between a primary part and a disowned part, as well as an underlying wounded part. Any strong reaction to something in your outside world is a warning signal that can tip you off that there is something going on inside you. This needs to be explored in order to be more in contact with your essence, to hear your soul's desire and to be more fulfilled.

Some questions that can help you discover primary, wounded and disowned parts in stressful situations are:

- What am I judging the other person of? (This can help you discover an unconscious disowned part: what you are judging the other person of is often an extreme version of a quality you disown, for example, being lazy is an extreme expression of being able to relax.)

- If I would allow myself to be more like that, what could I do or experience more of that would lead me to more fulfilment? (Integrating your disowned part helps you to become more fulfilled.)

- If I would allow myself to be more like that, what do I fear for myself? (This can help you discover an unconscious wounded part that is protected by your primary part, for example, fear of being insignificant, incompetent, unlikeable, judged, helpless.)

Using your outside world to develop more *self-awareness* of your inner parts that are blocking your soul's desire is the first step. *Self-compassion* for these parts is the next step because what you resist will persist. The final step to transformation and fulfilment is using *self-accountability* to balance these primary and disowned parts and to take care of your underlying wounded parts. For this third step, you can use conscious choice and repetition to override your old patterns and fears eventually. This might help in the short term or for minor patterns.

For stubborn patterns and for a deeper and longer-lasting change, you can use a variety of tools and techniques that help you transform the root cause of your inner imbalances and wounded parts. Self-awareness, self-compassion and self-accountability for your inner parts, which are mirrored by your outside world, allow you to respond more consciously and effectively to a situation, to listen deeper to your soul's desire, and to create a life of *success and fulfilment*.

MALOU LAUREYS

Malou Laureys lives in Gent, Belgium and works around the world as a master trainer, coach and therapist. She gets enormous joy out of inspiring people not only to be 'successful' leaders, but also to become 'soulful' leaders, creating meaning and fulfilment for themselves and the people around them.

She worked for 10 years in the corporate world as a civil engineer, manager and management consultant. In her search for fulfilment, she changed course and immersed herself for many years in psychology, psychotherapy, neuroscience, coaching and eastern philosophy, and started her own practice as a coach and therapist.

Today she combines her experience of the corporate world and the world of personal growth, to join entrepreneurs, executives, leaders and their teams on their journey to create and experience 'successful' *and* 'soulful' environments where effectiveness goes hand-in-hand with trust, authenticity, collaboration, purpose and fulfilment.

www.atransformationaljourney.com/
www.facebook.com/malou.laureys

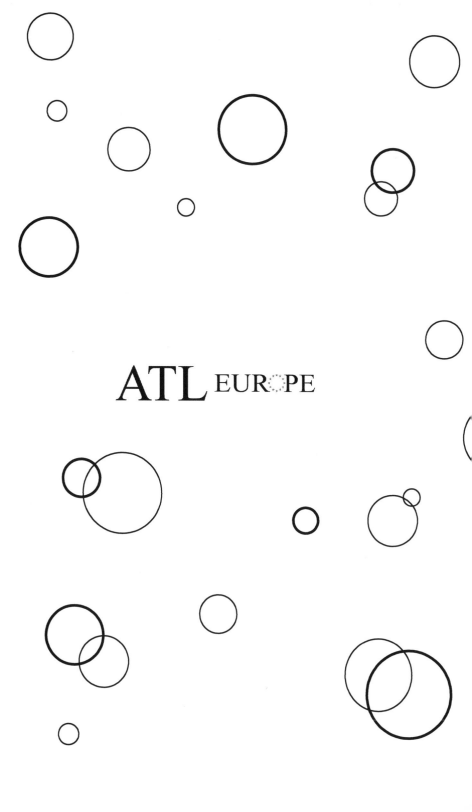

Chapter 24

A TIME TO CHANGE

Kezia Luckett

Have you ever got to a point in your life when you thought: "Is this it?

Is this all I've worked for, surely there must be more to life than this?

I've worked hard, I've followed the norm, I have gone over and above what is expected of me, but still I feel unfulfilled."

I was sitting indoors on a cold winter's day and these were the words I was hearing from one of my clients.

At the time, I was running an incredibly successful female-based concierge company helping busy professional mums juggle their work-life balance.

We were sitting in her home, a beautiful home for which she and her husband had worked hard. They had just renovated it, and it was so big that I often got lost walking around it. Both her children were in private school; her wardrobes were filled to overflowing with designer clothes, many with the tags still on; she had all the trappings of success that many people dream of, but here she was at home, when she should have been in her high-powered job in the city, signed off sick with depression.

As she carried on talking, I heard about anxiety attacks, of waking in the middle of the night wondering what had it all been for, but being scared to make a change. She had started looking outside herself, seeking books, people and transformational tools that she thought would help her find the way.

The scary thing was as I listened to her talk I knew that she wasn't alone. I was speaking to many clients who were feeling the same way, but worst of all, so was I.

The great Joseph Campbell described midlife as "reaching the top of the ladder and finding that it was against the wrong wall".

For me and for so many clients I spoke with, this summed it up. Even with all the external markers of success, we were unfulfilled, lacking purpose and not understanding the reason we had been put on this planet.

In his book, *The Seasons of a Woman's Life*, Daniel Levenson calls this the 'myth of the successful career woman'. The dream is that women can have it all – a happy family, a great career, great friends and live happily ever after – but what if this is not the case?

The period of midlife can often see us move away from societal, parental and marital expectations to a period of rediscovering ourselves, our dreams, our hopes and our desires. Although confusing, it can be one of the most spectacular and enlightening times in our lives.

It can be a time when we realise that the past has gone but a million possible futures are opening up. It's a time when that inner whisper starts to shout to be heard from within, a calling that gets louder and louder. A calling that can often leave you puzzled and confused: "Why me, who am I to make a change?"

But my question is: "Who are you not to?"

Will it be easy? Unfortunately, I cannot give you any guarantees, but when you feel that inner calling, shouting so loud, you must listen.

Mine came on a cold, wet, Boxing Day morning. I felt the calling to go for a walk in the pouring rain, so I donned my wet weather gear and headed out the door.

Within five minutes I was bombarded with images, visions, pictures and questions bubbling up from within. I tried to ignore it, but it got so loud and insistent I went home, sat in front of the computer and began to type.

After an hour had passed, I looked at what I had written and there on the screen was not only the idea for a worldwide movement that would ensure that every woman understood that they were good enough and that they could leave an impactful footprint on this world when they collaborated and shared their gifts with the world, but also the idea for a book that would show every woman that even something as simple as a story can pay forward and inspire, empower and change lives for the better.

Now you might think it was easy for me and that I wasn't scared, but I can tell you I was more frightened than I have ever been. I had to push against my husband, friends and family members who thought I had lost the plot, but I held the faith and belief that I was here to create a change in the world that had never been seen before and, come hell or high water, I was going to do it.

I knew that if I were to create a platform and community for change, it had to start with me. I needed to be better, do better and lead the way. As an introvert, the thought of stepping up and sharing my vision brought up the worst feelings ever. I had an internal debate in my head about being just an ordinary woman and I could never step up and be the change I wanted to see, but I have learned there is no such thing as ordinary.

We are all extraordinary women. No matter what you think right now, every interaction you have, every person you bump into, the way in which you view the world, makes you extraordinary. It is my mission to impact on one billion lives with *The Pay it Forward Series: Notes to My Younger Self* book and the Women of Contribution movement, to help women like you discover your true purpose and shine your light so bright for the world to see. I want to help you release the barriers and blocks of the past and fully step up, step in and be visible as the spectacular women you are, as you join forces with other women to collaborate and touch lives around the world. I truly believe that united we are strong, together we can make a difference – one woman at a time.

KEZIA LUCKETT

Kezia Luckett is an international bestselling author, motivational speaker, positive psychology coach and the CEO & Trailblazer behind the Women of Contribution movement.

When Kezia's life changed dramatically in 2016, following a vision to create a worldwide movement and community of contribution and collaboration, she already had more than 20 years' experience inspiring, empowering and supporting women through coaching and her work as an entrepreneur.

Through her *Pay It Forward Series: Notes to My Younger Self* books and platform, she coaches legacy entrepreneurs to step forward as leaders for change with one aim in mind: to impact on one billion lives worldwide.

Kezia is now on a mission to inspire all women to leave an impactful footprint through collaboration and sharing their gifts with the world. She knows that: "United we are strong. Together we can make a difference. One woman at a time."

www.womenofcontribution.com
www.facebook.com/groups/womenofcontribution

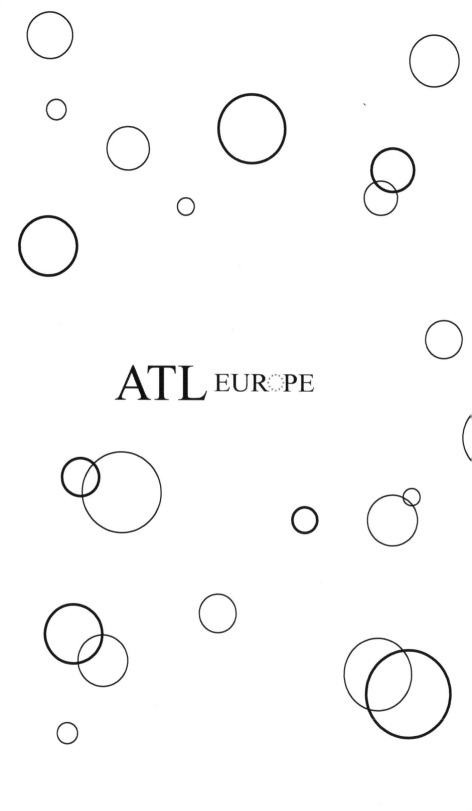

Chapter 25

SIMPLICITY OF PRESENCE

Jacinta Murray

You are in a time when your screens represent the most negative force. Your smartphones, computers and TV all take your time, energy and your presence. It is so easy to be distracted, yet your 'aha' or lightbulb moments happen only when you are present. There are many transformational shifts occurring for each of us. Old patterns are being relentlessly exposed to you. At times, you feel the freedom and the joy of being present. Then as a pattern exposes, you allow yourself to get distracted and sucked into a dense reality.

You have a force within that keeps you focused on what you are here to create, manifest, complete and share. When you are divinely present, manifestation and focus are effortless. So, you are getting frustrated, because what you are focusing on, manifesting, is not happening, and that it's not effortless, but effort filled.

Think about where all your attention goes. Everyone on social media knows that the biggest drain on your smartphone battery is Facebook. So, if you were a smartphone, who or what is the biggest drain on your internal battery. Who or what is diluting your focus, your ability to be present?

You can be present for others without losing your mind, your energy to your situations and issues. Being present, being love means you are a beacon, a source of comfort, with no loss of energy. Doing things resentfully because of a sense of duty or feelings of responsibility for others doesn't add to creating, to healing, to loving: it drains you of your life force and robs you of your peace of mind. There is a natural transformation occurring, aided by powerful celestial events: this is enough to deal with.

Time to stop diluting your life force, your goals, your abilities and be present, harness the force within and the unseen forces of support all around and be free to live in the light of your true self, loving, living, being.

These are times of intensity when your fears are being fuelled to erode your freedoms, and your issues are foremost in your reality. Every day, you need to remember the safest place to be during a storm is in the eye. You are experiencing more earthquakes, volcanic eruptions, solar flares, fires, flooding, and hurricanes. When it's not happening physically to you, you believe you are unaffected by events that are happening around the world. This is not so. The weather is occurring within humanity as much as it is occurring on the earth.

Everywhere you look: politics, institutions, workplaces and families are affected by implosions, explosions, separations, competition and divide and conquer. Many are experiencing flashes of anger, giving it or receiving it, extreme stress, or feelings of deep grief. The saying: "You teach people how to treat you" was never more relevant than it is now. You are being shown daily, through your interactions, areas where you are still lacking love for 'self'. Once you fully love and appreciate 'self', you no longer call in the lessons. Everyone respects you, and honours your truth, even if they don't agree with it.

The eye of the storm is the still point, and you are being reminded as the planet and humanity are experiencing tumultuous times, that to survive and thrive in the new normal of chaos, confusion, and creation you need to find that still point within. From that still point, you are present, you harness the power of the storm around you, you can create a new reality free of fear, and thrive.

There is no future in your past. Everything you have worried about, given excess energy to, has just drained you and wasted your time. So many times, you are still in the habit of worry: about others, about your health, wealth, work, mission, destiny and so on. Worry has been an endless infinite time-wasting reality of what ifs, and maybes, that you fed into. You jump into other people's minds and assume how they are thinking and use that assumption to put yourself down. You worry about being judged, which automatically gives everyone in your life the right to do so, because the minute you think about it, you create it, and feed it.

Now you are being given the opportunity to clear the pattern of habitual time-wasting worry from your psyche, and it is done by making 'the' choice 'that' it is over. Stop feeding worry and fear and they have no room to grow and spread. It is time to start feeding and nourishing you: by being present, you will experience a bountiful earth and a heart-driven society. When you feed fear you experience everything through that reality, and your life becomes small, tight, restrictive and life-taking.

When you become present, no thoughts predispose your position, everything just is. If something that's based on fear needs to be cleared, it presents to you, along with the solution, as long as you stay present to the gift without feeding the fear. When manifestation or creation needs to occur, then inspired action flows through.

When we create through fear or lack, everything is pushed away from you. Take a breath, be present in your universal flow. Allow yourself to be nourished, inspired and loved. Actions to be taken, to manifest the life of your choice, will flow into your mind effortlessly.

As an empath and (ex) people pleaser, it was only when I chose to be present that I truly felt the benefits. Synchronistic occurrences increased, and opportunities flowed. It is not a complex process: just make a choice and you will catch yourself quicker when you go into fear and then you will consciously return to the gift of your presence.

You now have a clear choice: you can perceive everything is mapped out, you can gurify, give your power away or, you can choose presence as your most wholesome state of being. Presence connects you to your eternal self and follows your heart's intelligence.

JACINTA MURRAY

Jacinta Murray is a keynote speaker, master teacher trainer, intuitive channel and life-force enhancer. She co-founded jacintachristy. com and the Divine Essence Crystal Healing Academy, and works closely with her husband Christy.

With 45 years' experience between them in metaphysics and healing methods, they are, as a husband and wife partnership, 'on-fire', inspired and ready to empower game-changers to reach their full potential. Being passionate spiritual teachers, they help those who are tired of conformity, to lead better, extraordinary and often exceptional lives.

They have worked on a conscious spiritual path for decades, facilitating empowerment events and personal sessions across the globe. They have also founded the Divine Essence Crystal Healing Academy, providing cutting-edge healing methods and training courses for aspiring spiritual teachers who want to make a difference too.

www.jacintachristy.com
www.divineessencecrystalhealing.com
www.instagram.com/jacintachristy/
www.facebook.com/jacintachristyMurray/?ref=bookmarks

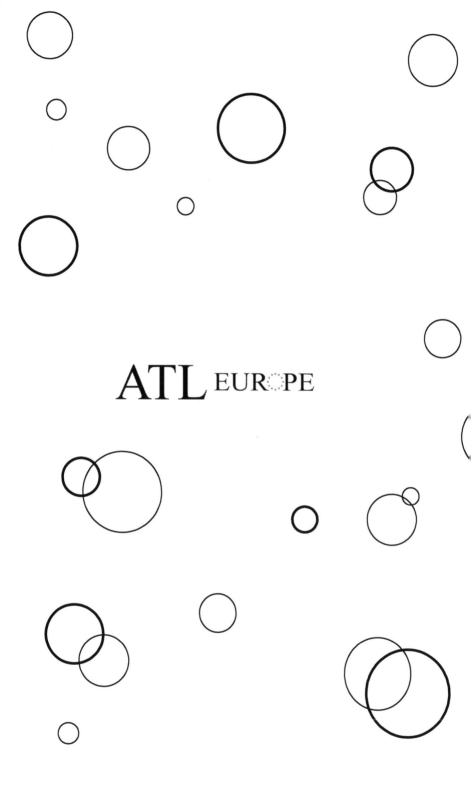

Chapter 26

YOUR FINANCIAL MINDSET

Izabella Niewiadomska

Have you ever worried about money, about not having enough to pay bills on time, paralysed by fear, afraid to make decisions?

Maybe you were earning more and yet your situation wasn't improving, and your credit card debts were increasing? Or perhaps you had a comfortable living, but no financial security and you felt scared about the future?

I know how it feels, because for a long time it was my reality. Then I found that life doesn't have to be this way, that I have the power to change it. You have this power too. I've made a lot of financial mistakes over the years. My belief was that 'money comes and money goes' and the state of my finances was reflecting exactly that belief. I was spending exactly what I had earned and sometimes more on credit and store cards.

Something had to change. I was now 30, a wife and a mother. My son was my biggest inspiration, my reason why. Soon I was presented with an opportunity to start a business. I had zero business experience, zero capital and yet I grabbed the opportunity with both hands. I saw it as hope for a better future. I started my own part-time business without a bank account or credit card and with a local payphone as my office.

Jim Rohn said: "If you want to be wealthy, study wealth." I became an eager student. I read *The Richest Man of Babylon, Think and Grow Rich* and others. I attended seminars with self-made millionaires and gradually things started improving, although not as fast as I could have wished for.

My business mentors introduced me to a concept that money is a tool and financial wealth is all about mindset. I kind of understood it. However, it took me a while to truly embrace this philosophy. It was a bit like hearing a song on the radio. You recognise the melody and think: "I know the song," and yet you can't sing it, because you don't know all the words.

Reading Robert Kiyosaki's *Rich Dad Poor Dad* taught me to focus on the language I was using, to turn statements into questions:

- From: I don't have enough money. I can't afford it.
- To: How can I have more money? How can I afford it?

It is the questions that force our brain to look for solutions, not the statements. One day I heard about David Hawkins' book, *Power vs Force*. Little did I know that this book would start me on the journey to completely transforming my life.

Its main message is that our thoughts create our reality. This means that if we adjust or change our thinking we have the power to adjust or change our reality. It was the message I needed to hear, because I just had lost some money trying to enter the property market.

Shortly afterwards, I was faced with a dilemma. I needed to attend a business leadership weekend in Lisbon and I was afraid that if I went I might not have enough money for my other financial commitments. That fear was holding me back. Should I stay, should I go?

Next morning, I woke up with a clear decision. A few minutes later, the doorbell rang. It was a postman with a recorded delivery letter. With a look of surprise, I opened a brown envelope addressed to me and found 100 lottery tickets inside. I got goosebumps! I dressed in a hurry and went to see how much I'd won. It was over £40! I was ecstatic! The amount didn't really matter. What mattered was that I had received money I hadn't expected.

It was a sign that I'd made the right decision, a decision based on abundance, not fear. I couldn't help but smile. I knew then that everything would be all right. I realised that when you trust, the universe will deliver, even from the most unexpected sources. It was my husband who had entered a *Daily Mail* competition and put my name on the form, so I would receive the prize.

The story doesn't end there. Just before I left for Lisbon, I received an email inviting me to the Chamber of Commerce the following week for the UK screening of a new movie, *The Secret*. The movie was related to the things I was reading about in that book. I reserved my ticket immediately.

On the night of the screening I was due to speak on a national conference call. I was going to miss the movie. How unfortunate, I thought. That was Wednesday. On Friday, another doorbell jump-started my day, with the arrival of another recorded delivery letter. This time it was from a friend in Australia. As I opened it, I was wondering what was inside. It was a DVD, a movie – *The Secret*! I watched it, mesmerised. I saw Marie Diamond, and didn't expect that 12 years later we would meet, become friends and contribute to the same book.

My relationship with money is completely different now from how it was 28 years ago when I moved from Poland to the UK.

I've learned that you, me and everyone else has access to the same powers and universal laws. They are at our disposal. The law of attraction, the power of thought, of choice, decision, gratitude – to mention just a few.

It is up to us to practise them daily, because only daily practice leads to mastery and transformation. Practising them has transformed my life – I'm happier, healthier and wealthier. I've learned to focus on a desired outcome and realised that worrying about money doesn't solve anything. It only brings more stress and health problems, and puts pressure on relationships.

The truth is, when you are truly grateful for all the money you have, for every amount you receive and when you believe that if today you have enough money for things you need, then you will always have enough money tomorrow. It works like magic, every single time.

Don't fear the future, create it the way you want. Live an inspired life.

IZABELLA NIEWIADOMSKA

Izabella Niewiadomska is a performance nutrition and wellness coach, health strategist, and international speaker. She founded Total Wellness and Nutritious Mind, was the nutrition sponsor for the World Record expedition and undertook a 100K ultra run to raise money for limbless veterans.

Winner of a Global Woman award and a Women of Contribution ambassador, Izabella is also a co-author of the international bestselling book, *Pay It Forward Series: Notes to My Younger Self*. Her new book is *Stop Dieting Start Eating – How to Look Delicious, Think Nutritious and Spice Up Your Life*.

After losing her health at 23, Izabella turned stress into resilience and delicious health. For 26 years she has been helping individuals and organisations with practical solutions that lead to a better health, high performance and an inspired life. She believes that what we eat, how we think and what we do daily has a major impact on our sustainable health, energy and happiness.

Featured in: *Women's Fitness, Top Santé, Global Woman, Daily Mail* and SKY TV.

www.izabellaniewiadomska.com
twitter.com/nutritiousmind
www.linkedin.com/in/izabellaniewiadomska
www.facebook.com/izabella.niewiadomska.7

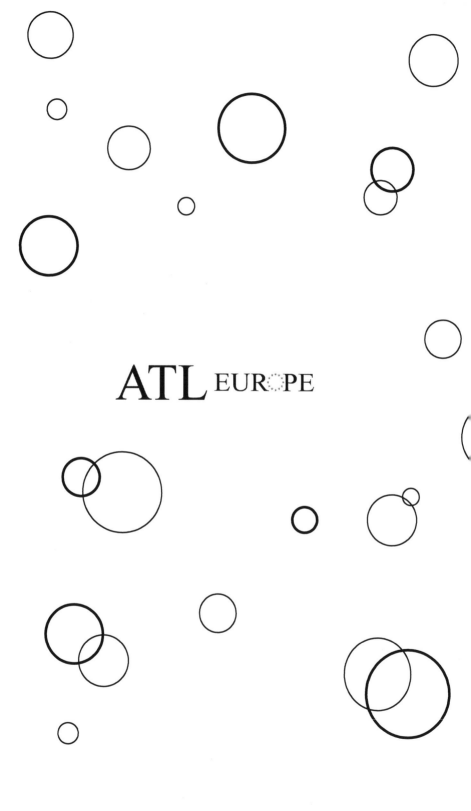

Chapter 27

BE CRAZY AND BRAVE – YOU WERE BORN TO BE ALIVE!

Sanja Plavljanić-Širola

I bet you are all familiar with the old disco song from the 70s by Patrick Hernandez: *Born To Be Alive*. Have you ever thought about those simple words? That the point of your life is to be alive? How alive do you feel?

Most of us feel aliveness in childhood and in teenage years. Afterwards, as the responsibilities pile up, our aliveness subsides and many people start spending their days 'on autopilot', 'just managing' or 'getting through'.

But you were not born to 'endure' your life: you were born to be *alive*! To wake up with a sparkle in your eyes and a song in your heart, to follow your passions and share your gifts. And to explore how far and wide you can go, what you can do and be and how you can contribute to making the world a better place.

What makes one feel alive? Courageously following your heart's desires. Daring to fully become your unique, wonderful and crazy self. Do you also love Frank Sinatra's song: *My Way*? Everybody does. We all know how good it feels to create your life your own way.

How I became alive

Does your profession define you forever? Why would you develop only one side, one set of skills and talents? You are full of different treats and it is a pity to neglect them.

As long as your profession is making you happy and alive, stick to it, but if you start feeling unhappy and unsatisfied – it is time for change. Don't ever try to persuade yourself that you *should* feel happy if you are just not.

For 20 years, I was an architect and mostly loved that profession. I had many other interests, too. There came a time, in my early 40s, when I started feeling unhappy. My heart was whispering: "I want to do something else!" And my mind was replying: "Don't be ridiculous, you were educated for architecture, you are good at it, what else would you do? Besides, you have clients, employees, the office with computers and printers – you can't destroy that!"

For a while, I listened to my mind, trying to feel better. But it didn't work. I was just not feeling *alive*. So, I decided to figure out what could I become, that would make my heart really happy. I had no clue. First, I allowed myself to believe that my ideal profession existed and was available for me.

Second, I let go of the attachments to my role as an architect. I decided to follow my heart's impulses when they felt clear.

One spring day in 2007 I suddenly got an impulse: "I want to meet the author of my favourite book, *Your Heart's Desire* – Sonia Choquette." I immediately searched for her workshops online and found the Caribbean cruise organised by Hay House that autumn. I had never been on a cruise and did not have enough money for it, but it sounded like an exciting idea. My heart said: "Go!"

So, I took the third step – 'crazy' move: I made the reservation for myself and kids, and paid for it, believing I would earn the rest by autumn.

At that time, my marriage was in crisis and I had no savings, but I trusted my heart. I didn't listen to the 'common sense'. Common sense is sometimes just nonsense. And the crazy move that sounded like a nonsense, turned out to lead me to my life purpose.

Autumn arrived, and we went on the cruise. And this wonderful adventure has subsequently led to a chain of events (and 'crazier' moves) that completely changed my life.

I soon closed my office and became a teacher, helping people follow their hearts and make their dreams come true. I have been doing this for 10 years now, enjoying it immensely. My new job has brought me to a lot of amazing world destinations and connected me to so many wonderful people – filled my heart with joy and made me feel more *alive* than ever. And my marriage became happy again, too.

So, forget about 'One day I will...'

Do you have a longing to change something in your life, to live differently? To feel more *alive*?

What are you waiting for? You can never be perfectly prepared: perfection comes as you walk your new path. And the things you are afraid to lose are most probably the very things that don't make you happy. And what the others will think? Whoever really loves you will be happy to see you happy. So please, finish this sentence: One day I will...

_____

_____

That day is today. The right moment for change is – now. Don't wait, start moving in your desired direction.

Courage evokes magic

It takes courage to live your life your own way. But, here is the great news: *Courage sets magic into motion.* When you fill your wings with courage and make a bold step, you initiate the sequence of miracles – the doors start opening and new opportunities appear. So, here is a new task.

If I had more courage, I would:

_____

_____

Decide to have that courage. Every day of your life. Create your life under your own terms, create your own world.

Transformational lesson

You are born to be alive. If you don't feel happy where you are, it means you need to be someone else or somewhere else. Listen to your heart's whisper. Do the things that make your heart sing.

Your dream life is possible. Allow yourself to dream it.

Dare to do your own thing, even if no one has done it before, even if you have no proof that it will work, even if nobody understands it. And the magic will unfold. And don't worry, if you stand firmly by who you really are, everybody will accept it. Be crazy, be awkward, be different, be an example. It is your life. Be *alive!*

SANJA PLAVLJANIĆ-ŠIROLA

Sanja Plavljanić-Širola spent 20 years as an architect, running her own practice. Following having undertaken training in alternative disciplines (four-year school for integrative therapists, *Snowlion*, five-year feng shui academy, eight of Sonia Choquette's USA workshops) in 2008 she summoned the courage to change profession: she became a workshop teacher and a therapist.

Sanja owns the centre for personal development, Sretan dan, in Zagreb, Croatia, which has more than 1.000 students and individual clients. Sanja's biggest passion is helping people to courageously follow their hearts and discover the magic of the universe. She loves lighting up forgotten inner sparks.

Sanja is a columnist for zivim.hr portal and a magazine, *Vita*. In Croatia she published a booklet, *A-HA thoughts*, and her new book and workbook, *Living in the Flow of Magic*, will be soon translated to English.

She has been a member of ATL Europe since 2015, and is married, with two grown-up sons.

http://sanjasirola.me/
sretan-dan.hr/
www.facebook.com/sanja.plavljanicsirola

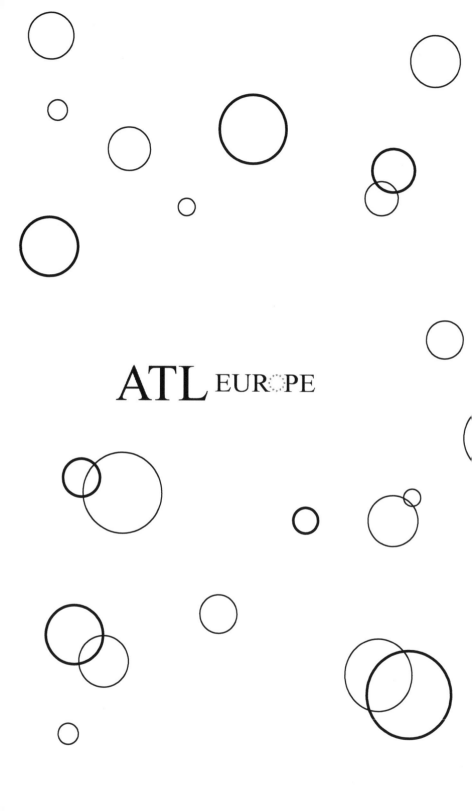

Chapter 28

THANK YOU, GRATITUDE FOR SAVING MY LIFE

Ivana Plechinger

My stroke – a stroke of luck!

I had a stroke. At the age of 39. Early on I thought that could happen only to 'old people' in their 60s. I survived. Now I am even more headstrong than before. As I left the hospital, doctors told me I was in perfect health and that it was all caused by stress. Indeed. Were you ever told by a doctor that your health issues are caused by stress? Thought so. We have all heard it. Headlines are screaming: "Stress is the illness of our times."

My stress was called 'we took a home loan with no steady income' and 'I am losing one job with no other within reach yet.' Is that what I nearly died for and what could have deprived my sons of their mother, my husband of his wife, and the world of the phenomenal me? Good job, Ivana.

I came home dragging along the dark thoughts proverbially present in everyone who encounters a severe diagnosis. Neither my husband nor the children recognised me in such a depressive state and I didn't fancy myself either when I was so dark. I have been a blonde all my life, what is this? Fortunately, that Ivana irritated me immensely and I was looking for ways to gently push her out of my life, for her motto, "If this happens to me again I'll hurt myself," has never been my motto.

For years I had been devouring self-help books, mostly because I hate to iron, and because I adore Oprah Winfrey. Let me watch her show and I'll iron your carpet if need be! Every book she recommended I began to absorb right away, without knowing why spirituality attracted me.

Today I know I was preparing to survive everything life put in my way since 2012, for I am the living proof that a wise book can literally save one's life. In the fight against that snivelling me, I was first helped by the realisation that my mother had died of cancer at the age of 39. She was gone, yet at that same age I had survived. Yes. That is how literal things must be in my life. Your typical blonde!

There has to be a more profound meaning to my survival other than just living on and fearing the next stroke. I won the second round against the depressive me when I remembered the cult book by the phenomenal Louise Hay, *You Can Heal Your Life*. It contains a chart showing what can cause certain illnesses on a spiritual level and under *stroke* it says: fear of the future. I froze! I never feared the future as I did prior to my stroke. When I learned that fear is in fact stress and when I related that to what I'd been told how my falling ill was due to stress, I knew I was on the right track. Thank you, Louise, you have helped me immensely, as you did a host of others.

Thank you, gratitude for saving my life

We are governed by only two basic emotions: fear and love. All our feelings stem from them. I realised I would keep away from fears and hospitals the more I loved. But how to achieve that?

Everything you need comes at the right moment and a sentence materialised before my eyes that all the good in the world derives from gratitude. Earlier I had thought exactly the opposite, that *one must be happy to begin with in order to feel gratitude* for happiness. Not so. Be grateful first in order to appreciate every second of your life! The concept of gratitude for everything that I have or would have seemed strange, but I had nothing to lose. All I wanted was to knock out the depressive me once and for all so I embraced 'violence', the only kind I can tolerate. Being unaccustomed to it I began to think 'violently' and changed my life to the core! Mundane and yet so powerful and I wish to pull you along, my friend.

I faced every morning with a 'must' and those 'must-do chores' made me tired even before I got up. From then on, I began every morning by thanking for something for at least a minute, from small things like 'for my soft bed', 'for warm water', 'for the inventor of boiler'. If there are great things to be grateful for, so much the better: "Thank you for my wonderful children," "Thank you for my husband who loves me even when I am not lovable," and "Thank you because I am living my dream."

You will notice your day begins differently, you'll feel uplifted and in the day ahead you will find more new reasons for gratefulness. Soon a minute each morning won't suffice because of so many new reasons for gratefulness. It feels so powerful to be grateful for what you still only wish to experience. Pre-emptive gratitude. May *this* force be with you.

Try to apply everything mentioned for the next 40 days and notice the change in your life. If there is an improvement – please never stop it.

I haven't, and that is how I managed to stay strong after the sudden death of my beloved father, I had another chance to be grateful when my elder son nearly got killed recently after being hit by a police car at the pedestrian crossing. I kept saying: "Thank you God for watching over him." The universe does not understand our words, only vibrations, and gratitude is the supreme vibration.

Please don't take my word for it but rather try it and see for yourself. And from now on, every morning I shall express my gratitude for your decision, my friend, to let all the happiness in the world into your life.

Thank you for that.

IVANA PLECHINGER

After becoming a pop star at the age of 19, Ivana Plechinger hosted a children's TV show for years and now works at Croatia's most listened to radio station.

At the age of 39 she suffered a stroke that shook her to the core, as did the sudden death of her father, to whom she was very attached.

She took up writing and her husband encouraged her to offer her book for publishing, which was welcomed by all the publishers she contacted. *At the End of the Way Only Love Will Stay* immediately became a bestselling book in Croatia and will soon be published in Serbia as well.

Ivana toured the country and started her weekly YouTube programme relating the beauty of life, followed closely by the entire region.

She is a facilitator, motivational speaker and lecturer and only now does she seem to be living what she was born to do.

www.ivanaplechinger.com
https://www.youtube.com/channel/UC0i95zJjR6Y9iJ-GtMh2y0w
YouTube Ivana Plechinger English channel

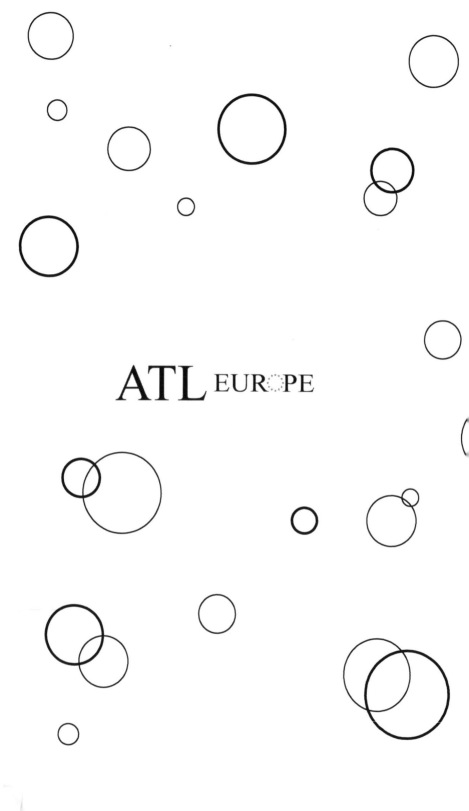

Chapter 29

SEIZING THE OPPORTUNITY OF A LIFETIME

Jan Polak

Changing times, fundamental challenges

An old Chinese proverb says: "May you live in interesting times." And we do. We live in a fascinating era marked by prosperity, unprecedented opportunities and technological progress. But we also live in times of ever-greater external distractions and internal confusion, suffering and pressure.

Despite it being probably the best time ever to live on Earth, most of us are not satisfied with how we live and how we work. Particularly, the work we do and organisations we are involved with can prove challenging and frustrating. We know we are falling short of what is possible.

We seek an environment and an avenue at work to not just earn a living but to be ourselves, to fully develop our potential, to enjoy what we are doing, productively spend time with people that inspire us, achieve results that we care about and prosper without living at the expense of our human essence and the future generations.

Is it possible at all?

We all share a full spectrum of human needs that we grow into over time and that go from ego-based (survival, acceptance, self-esteem) to soul-based (self-realisation, making a difference, and selfless service). Is it possible to express all these needs in and through business?

At a young age, I experienced fabulous success as a well-paid business professional. The world was my oyster. I travelled on business, stayed at the best hotels and dined at the best restaurants. I met fascinating and influential people. And I also had a chance to be part of projects that changed the way corporations and industries worked, and affected the lives of thousands of people whom I didn't know.

After a few fleeting moments of feeling proud and accomplished, however, I often experienced a sense of emptiness or fear that I might not be able to keep it up or even lose what I had so painstakingly achieved. External success came at great personal cost.

For a short period of time I also tried a different approach. I learned equally painfully that giving up on my dreams, avoiding responsibility, and accepting mediocrity was definitely not a way of life, work and doing business that would inspire me to jump out of my bed every morning.

I started pondering whether it was possible to integrate the apparent polarities of everyday work life – to reconcile achievement and fulfilment, joy and productivity, business and humanity – and how to be a part of something larger without losing myself.

What makes a difference?

To get new insights and answers, I needed to start asking new questions and above all question existing answers.

I found that we need to shift our perspective at three levels: how we see ourselves, others, and business itself, and this is what provides the essence of the work I do now with entrepreneurs and business clients around the world.

a) Bring your unique self to work

We work best when we are at our best. Not when working hard trying to comply or impress. To be more than just replaceable cogs in a machine, we need to find our uniqueness and bring it to work.

We all have a set of talents that enable us to carry out certain activities naturally and with ease; passions that reflect our enthusiastic interest and energise us; as well as values and maybe even a sense of mission we are willing to live and die for that give a sense of purpose.

Our uniqueness is often hidden from us in plain sight, and hence we may fail to see how valuable it can be under the right conditions at work or generally in business. Once we discover our uniqueness and bring it to the table, work becomes joyful and fulfilling as well as productive.

b) Foster fruitful collaboration

Everything around us is built on collaboration. It acknowledges our interdependence in society, economy, and at work. And our uniqueness comes alive, strengthens and expands in collaboration.

Extraordinary collaboration leads to extraordinary results. When we let go of our fear of not having or being enough, when we stop competing for attention, position or credit, and pull behind a common goal, we get into flow and miracles happen.

c) Focus on meaningful contribution

What gives fuel to collaboration and what gives meaning to business – whether you are a small entrepreneur or a large corporation – is not focusing on maximising profit but maximising our potential, impact and contribution to others.

Money is an important indicator of value and provides nutrients for healthy functioning and growth. However, making money the main goal is limiting and dangerous. As we eat to fully live and do not live to eat, so our businesses and organisations could thrive by making money as a means of connecting and developing people to serve humanity.

Mission possible

Transforming the way we work and do business is a formidable task. You may ask whether it is even possible. What can one person do? Where do I start? As individuals, we can start by recognising and following our own uniqueness and engaging it where it adds most value.

This means having the courage to choose jobs and roles that help you apply your natural talents, engage with your passion, live in accordance with your values and meaningfully contribute on a daily basis. Indeed, there was never a greater need in business for people who authentically bring their best selves to work.

As business owners or leaders, you have an opportunity to design and direct your businesses in such a way that people will be inspired and attracted to work with you. Isn't it a great opportunity to be the one who provides exactly the environment people are already looking for and want to be a part of? This shift is not only possible, it is worthwhile. Transforming how we work is the opportunity of our lifetime. What remains is only to wholeheartedly seize it. That might be the mission for you, should you choose to accept it.

JAN POLAK

Jan Polak is a pioneer of a new business paradigm and purpose-led and values-driven business.

He is a consultant, mentor and coach of business leaders, entrepreneurs and their teams with international experience in the UK, USA, Australia, South Africa, India, Hong Kong, the Czech Republic and Slovakia.

An advocate for an integral approach to business, Jan empowers entrepreneurs and business leaders to build and lead organisations that prosper by making a difference in the world. Jan's particular expertise lies in the facilitation of organisational mission and culture alignment, and the development and use of human potential and synergistic collaboration in small, medium and large companies.

Previously Jan worked as a management consultant with McKinsey & Company and as a partner in the London-based Strategy Dynamics Solutions Ltd. He holds an MBA from London Business School and a master's in Industrial and Labor Relations from Cornell University specialising in organisational behaviour.

www.janpolak.com
www.linkedin.com/in/janpolak/
twitter.com/JanPolak

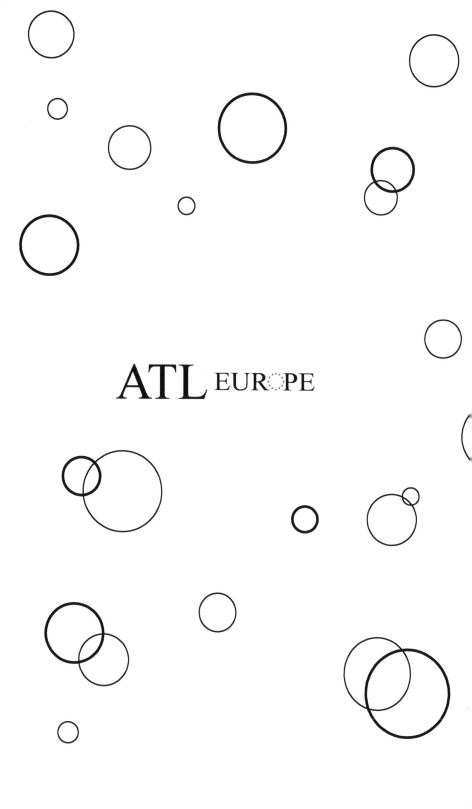

Chapter 30

UNLEASH YOUR LEADERSHIP THROUGH OPERA

Patrick Pype

My mission in life is to enable people to find and radiate their uniqueness in this world. I accomplish this by giving seminars, sharing my insights in books and coaching corporate leaders based on opera fragments.

My background is being a top manager in the technology industry for more than 30 years. At the same time, I am a big fan of opera. From that perspective, the idea grew to realise a cross-fertilisation between these two worlds of opera and leadership.

The idea of opera leading to new views on leadership might seem strange. It is indeed something special, but it is not only me who is passionate about it: for example, Roland Cracco, managing director of Interparking, mentions in the magazine of the Brussels opera house De Munt how opera inspires him when making decisions.

Transformation means the evolution from a person who is 'managing according to the classical management books' towards 'managing according to his/her true beliefs'. It is the evolution from a target-driven way of working towards a coaching and managing 'from the heart' approach, in which creating trust and demonstrating permanent personal integrity is a key asset.

I can illustrate this in my career, which consists of four main steps. At the beginning of my career, I felt like the Parsifal character in Richard Wagner's opera. I didn't have any real-life experience. I had only my theoretical knowledge on project management. I considered myself an 'innocent fool' at the very beginning. I jumped into managing projects without taking into account the feelings and emotions of the people I managed. I only looked at targets and goals: "Within two years, we need to have that result."

The first step consisted of the evolution from 'target setter' to 'people manager'. I evolved from being too directive a leader into a true people manager.

The second step was to evolve from 'people manager' to 'personal growth'. When you grow personally, you also 'feel' the team better instead of just managing it.

The third step was the evolution of 'personal growth' to 'team growth'.

My last (and current) step was to evolve from 'being an actor' to 'being my true self'.

Instead of always having a big smile when entering a meeting or banning emotions during discussions, I became increasingly convinced that people want to see a real person, not a theatre player. My main evolution was to make decisions from my inner self, combining facts and intuition, instead of looking solely at facts. An important asset is to do permanent self-reflection, as this will lead to new insights. Sometimes it is better to stand still instead of running the daily rat race.

I realised that the insights I gained during my whole career and my growth towards becoming a transformational leader, did not come only from the pure job execution and experience. It also came from my cultural experiences in opera, where I suddenly found out that there is a link between what happens on the opera stage and what happens in a business environment.

Over a number of years this influence took place in an unconscious way, but suddenly it became conscious and even had more influence. It formed the basis of seeing situations at work more clearly through the rational and emotional scenes which take place in the opera.

Based on the wisdom in opera, I found new insights into my own evolution from 'innocent fool' to 'transformational leader':

- Realistic expectations motivate all

- Maintain integrity and never compromise

- Trust others, but trust yourself first

- Balance your heart and mind

- Stick to your beliefs in spite of resistance

- Master your ego and empower

- Become your true self

- Continuous self-reflection leads to new insights

And for people who feel reluctant about looking to an opera and who do not understand how opera can give new insights into their daily leadership activities, let me quote Pascal Mercier: "Curiosity is the power to let you be prisoned by the unknown and through this get liberated from the burden of your feelings from history" (The Piano Tuner, 2008).

Tips of Transformation:

I ask you to give a yes or no answer to a few statements below so you can assess how much of a transformational leader you are:

- I am 100% sure that I never show any inconsistent behaviour.

- In order to make a decision, I bring together all arguments and investigate pros and cons. If I lack some information I will not go for an intuitive decision, but will keep gathering all the rational elements available as the basis for a final decision.

- Once I have made a decision, I go for it and never look back.

- I prefer to work with people who follow me blindly, rather than with those who keep on questioning every decision made.

- As a leader, you have to play a role of motivating and empowering people, and you often have to forget to show your emotions or to be your real self.

If you have answered 'yes' to all these statements, you might be a transformational leader, but you are probably not (yet). You are wondering why? Because a truly transformational leader is not always 100% sure of an answer to a question. You can doubt and you can use intuitive feelings for making a decision instead of trying to get 100% of the information on the table. Furthermore, self-reflection is a key characteristic of a transformational leader.

So, on your path to the final goal, you will take time to stand still, reflect and see whether the proposed path forward is still the best one or whether changes are needed. It is sometimes good that other people question you about a certain decision, provided that it does not happen all the time and that it does not create a negative atmosphere or too much delay. A 'transformational leader' can realise 'transformations' only by being a human being and not by playing a 'theoretical perfect leader-role'. My main tip is to dare to get out of your comfort zone and keep reflecting on it.

PATRICK PYPE

Patrick Pype was born in Roeselare, Belgium in 1962. He studied electrical engineering and attained an MBA at the University of Leuven (KULeuven). He has more than 30 years' worldwide management experience (IMEC, CoWare, Philips and NXP), managing teams in Europe, India and Silicon Valley.

He has been a speaker at several conferences and is currently leading a €50m+ cooperation project with 150 people from 69 different partners (including industry, research institutes and universities), spread over 16 countries throughout Europe.

He was chairman of the engineering alumni association from the KULeuven and a board member of the overall KULeuven Alumni Association (Alumni Lovanienses).

He co-created ATL Europe, an international non-profit association with members throughout Europe, which is sharing experiences of transformational leadership among members and throughout Europe.

Patrick's main hobby is attending opera performances all over Europe. He has published a book showing how the opera world can lead to new insights in transformational leadership.

www.patrickpype.eu
www.linkedin.com/in/patrickpype/
www.facebook.com/patrick.pype

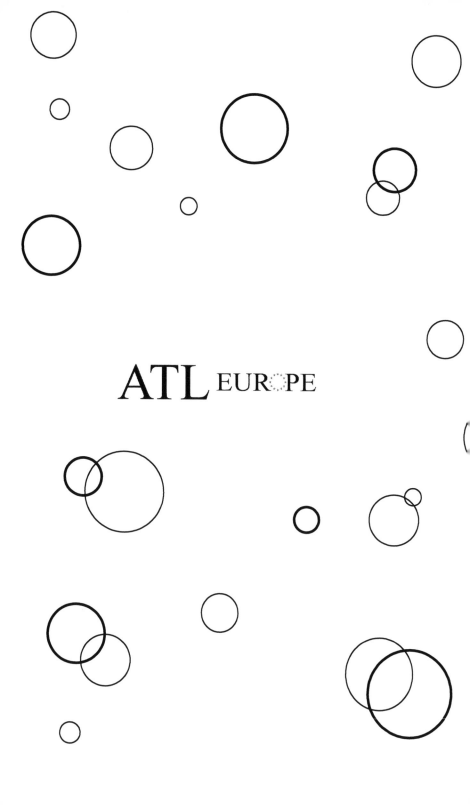

Chapter 31

THE POWER OF YOUR WHOLE VOICE

Judith Quin

When you connect your voice to your body, and your brain to your higher purpose, you can liberate your voice from the fears of rejection or judgment; and speak to others with clarity, confidence, and conviction.

Unfortunately, too many people go through life either feeling unable to express themselves, overcome with nerves, or speaking with a voice that is disconnected from who they really are. This disconnection is physical, mental and emotional and you might be surprised how it affects all kinds of people in all areas of life, personal and professional.

The first time *I* discovered that I restricted my voice was in a voice class at drama school – repeating a specific sound unleashed a flood of frustration, then tears. When I embraced the sound, there was a whole new depth, richness and openness to my voice. I didn't realise, until I discovered sound healing, quite how much I held on to. Learning to embrace the whole of my voice has brought another whole level to my life and that is why I'm passionate about sharing the practice.

The power of sound is that, as sound waves travel through you, they resonate with the energy from which you created your disconnection. When you reconnect to your *whole* voice vibration, you can release the fears and find a new perspective, empowering you to be both seen and heard.

Physical disconnection

It's likely that in situations you find challenging, you reduce the amount of your body that is supporting your voice. Maybe you always speak like this. This is a physical response to your mental and emotional holdings and restrictions. It can manifest as a voice that sounds trapped, quiet, or mumbled, or a body that betrays you through nerves.

To transform these patterns, you need to reconnect your voice to your body. Breathe fully; feel how your body responds, your belly and ribs expanding and contracting: this is the first step to finding your physical voice.

Now let your sound vibration resonate; hum, feel the vibration in your body – if you find tones that shut down, feel frustrating, or emotional, you've started to open up the physical spaces you've disconnected from, which hold ...

Mental disconnection

In childhood, you created beliefs about yourself, which you either consciously, or subconsciously, still hold. For example, if you believe 'it's bad to show off' when you speak in front of others, your body probably tries to make you appear smaller and your voice unclear or quiet. Your brain disconnects from the truth of who you are and how that benefits others, focusing instead on what you *believe*.

The other mental disconnection is where you replace what's *really* important with focusing on the immediate need, or lack, in your life. For example, you think: "I need to sign this client because I need the money." This does have purpose, but if you were thinking: "I want to build a good relationship with this client so I can help them develop," that is a *higher* purpose (and will probably make you more money in the long run too.)

In personal relationships this could be: "I need to let you know how angry I am" over "I want this relationship to last, but need to let you know how you hurt me, so we can grow."

Start replacing your mental disconnection thoughts (such as: "I'm not good enough," "Why would they listen to me?", or "I don't like this") with more beneficial ones (such as "I know my subject," "My ideas are valid," or "If I share this, I might help someone"). Your audience will hear the difference.

Emotional disconnection

This is your body and voice's reaction to emotional hurt or judgment that you previously felt in life when you expressed yourself. In the same way that muscle memory helps you remember how to ride a bike, your cells remember your emotional hurts. When you are in a situation that feels as though it might expose you to similar emotional 'danger', your body responds by not allowing your voice access to areas that might expose vulnerability, so, in turn, your voice closes down.

Releasing emotional restrictions can feel challenging: humans get strangely attached to their pain. When you discover areas in your voice that feel vulnerable, try making sounds around that thought, feeling, or space in your body. Remind yourself that the situation that originally created the emotional block was when you were younger. What you perceived as a hurtful intention may not have been intended by the perpetrator – even if it was, you are not the same person any more.

Whether physical, mental, or emotional, the blocks you hold around sharing your voice are from a younger different version of you; from beliefs that may or may not be true. These restrictions take energy to hold on to. Sound is energy: it connects you to your physical and energetic bodies; and matching the vibrational energy of your restrictions can also help you release them. This is why sound is a beautifully gentle, and effectively direct and powerful, method of transformation.

Start to explore, expand, and accept your voice vibration: you may recognise, or release, some of your restrictions.

Start humming: play with your sound up and down in tone and feel the vibration you create. Where you find an area that feels stuck, gently make notes a little higher or lower than the one that recognised the emotion or feeling, and let your sound explore what it might feel like to inhabit that space. Start to accept your voice back where it belongs.

My transformational message for you

You are no longer the younger version of you who, for whatever reason, felt that you did not deserve to be seen or heard. You have a voice; it's OK to be seen. When you speak, it is not about *you*, but about the effect, or result you want to create – so take a breath, ground, connect to your higher purpose, and speak.

JUDITH QUIN

In Peru, in 2013, Judith worked with shaman Elisa Varda, who said "Your voice is your gift, Judith. You must share it."

Judith created *Your Whole Voice* as a vocal-liberation method for high-purpose people who want to share *their* voice. Working holistically, Judith knows the value of looking at the whole picture: everything creates a ripple, and words make waves. By combining her acting and coaching skills, and using the power of sound and voice vibration, she connects you to who you really are, liberating your voice by illuminating the truth of your 'Higher purpose'.

Judith changes people's lives, by changing their mindset around expressing themselves, liberating them from old life-patterns physically, mentally and emotionally. She gives you the tools to create what you want to say, and how to say it, with greater clarity, confidence and conviction.

Judith is also an international public speaker and author of *Stop 'Should-ing'. Start Wanting.*

www.YourWholeVoice.com
www.facebook.com/yourwholevoice
twitter.com/YourWholeVoice

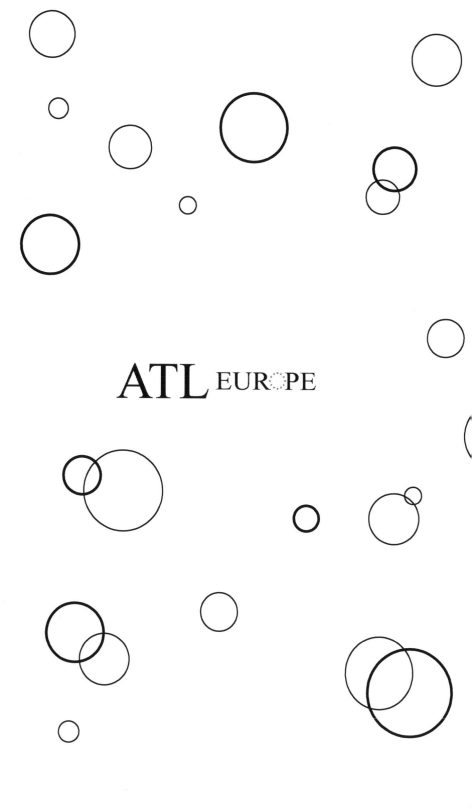

Chapter 32

WOMEN HAVE A DIFFERENT WAY OF DOING BUSINESS FROM MEN. WHY IS THEIR WAY SO DIFFERENT?

Tineke Rensen

For example, 66% do not create an annual plan for their business. And 60% do not create financial budgets.

I decided to research the female way of doing business. Why? My competitors were all male business owners. So, I learned to do business the male way. I saw that women used a different style, and I had to conclude that their way was less successful according to my definition, which was money-oriented, the same as that of my male opponents.

How women do business

After I sold my first international business, I wondered why female-owned businesses overall remained so small. I did see the potential of female business owners, but often their businesses remained too small to make any difference in the world.

After a while, I decided to investigate the female way of doing business and I questioned nearly 400 female business owners. My detailed report of this study, *How Women do Business*, is available on my website.

Naturally, women are lacking the skills that make men successful in business. Off course there are women who have a lot of masculine energy or skills and often they are more successful than other women. What are typical masculine skills that make business owners successful?

Men naturally:

- Like to compete

- Have focus

- Are system thinkers and a business is a system if you manage it well

- See more and bigger opportunities

- Are not afraid to take risks

- Are goal-oriented

- Keep a good overview of the whole process

- They love the speed of implementation

- Dare to promote themselves if this helps the business

- Say yes before they know how to do it

- Like to negotiate

Apparently, this behaviour works, although many women don't like these skills, or don't know how to do it. I was surprised to discover that there is a feminine way of doing business too. I thought there was only one successful way of doing business. And most books (written by male authors) endorsed my opinion of doing business in a successful way.

What my male opponents often said about female business owners was:

- Their businesses are too small

- They do not dare to position themselves very well
- They do not seem to have faith in their own product or service because they are insecure
- I cannot level with them in a conversation

And ladies, sorry if I offend you, I was thinking exactly the same. Because I was doing business the masculine way, I discovered something shocking about doing business.

We think everybody has equal chances in business, but I strongly disagree. The language of men is spoken. Their behaviour is accepted.

And their way of doing business is common.

Only 1% of the big business deals in the corporate world are going to female-owned businesses (source: We-Connect).

Women who adopt the masculine skills are more accepted and are often more successful. They often become a business owner, as I used to be. I adopted the masculine way of thinking, communicating and doing business. This was great when I did business with men. But it didn't work so well with women. They did not 'feel' me. They did not want to see the successful image that I created. They wanted to see the real me. And guess what?

I had no clue, because I did not accept my femininity I thought femininity was weak. I had no clue how wrong I was at that time.

What's strong about women in business?

And why their businesses need to grow!

It was only two years ago that I discovered what is so strong about female-owned businesses.

- They hardly ever go bankrupt

- Their business *always* delivers (a woman will not say yes if she is not convinced she can deliver)

- Most staff like to work a lot for female-owned businesses

- Women often don't need to have facts, they can trust their gut feeling

- They are very creative

- For them, the relationship is more important than the money

- They are very thorough

- They can easily find consensus. They are not convinced that their way is the best

- Their services and products are of high quality

And I hope you agree with me that these kinds of skills are needed very much in the world right now.

What I learned from women and men

The things we don't like so much about men in business are exactly those skills that we need to adopt. And we can do that the feminine way.

We can take a year planning and take into account our relationships and work on a better service or product at the same time.

Women can grow their businesses faster if we brag about ourselves or the business. We think it is bragging, but most of the time it is absolutely true. Women underestimate and undervalue themselves tremendously.

Women have to spend a little more time to understand finances. In general, our brains are not wired to understand this very easily. If we do though, it gives us more control. We can speed up a lot faster if we also focus on numbers and not only on relationships.

We need to have more focus because we are aware of everything that is going on around us. That does not mean we need to act on everything we are aware of.

Women tend to forget their goals when they get too specific or precise. Timeframes are there to protect us from getting lost in perfectionism.

It is good to see and feel everything when relationships are concerned but don't do this with your financial targets. This is about numbers, statistics, and facts.

Where do you start?

Surround yourself with strong and feminine business women.

Read the right books, written by women.

Find female role models such as the author of *Butterfly in a Storm*: Giselle Rufers.

Join a strong women's network.

Seek help. Invest in yourself. This will definitely be an investment that will last forever.

TINEKE RENSEN

In 1990, Tineke Rensen was the only female entrepreneur in her industry, so she learned to do business the masculine way. It is a successful way. She also became a national kayaking champion. When she encountered women, she saw that they had a different approach. It did not match her definition of success, which was very masculine.

When she started to develop her feminine skills in business, she saw another definition of success. She soon realised that a combination of the masculine and feminine approaches was the best way to achieve success in business. She also saw that many women needed to improve the masculine skills to get the business they desired.

So she sold her business and started teaching this to businesswomen all over the world. She founded the Powerful Business Women's Network and wrote a book, *Maximum Business Growth for Women*. She is passionate to speak about this topic on international stages.

www.PowerfulBusinessWomensNetwork.com
www.MaximumBusinessGrowthforWomen.com
www.MeetTinekeRensen.com
www.PowerfulBusinessAcademy.com

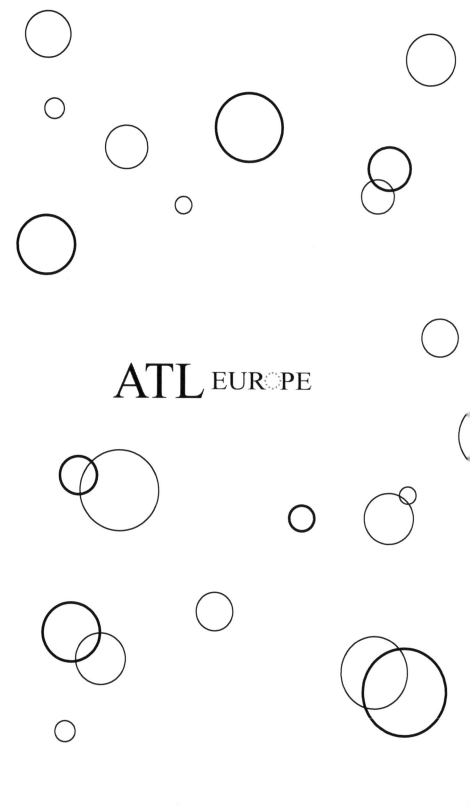

Chapter 33

PROJECT HEAVEN ON EARTH: CREATING AND LIVING OUR NEW HUMAN STORY

Martin Rutte

Enough already! The significant problems we're facing aren't being solved: wars drag on, millions suffer severe drought and famine, ice caps melt, global financial markets are unstable, terrorism continues. Even our moral bastions are in trouble — witness the abuse scandals in religious institutions.

Add to this the underlying belief that we as individuals can't make any impactful difference, not just in making these situations better, but in ending them. The prevailing sense is that none of us can make a difference, that one individual can't take on a suffering – war, hunger, disease – and end it. One individual can't take on an institution – government, the financial industry, religion – and really make it work. There's nothing we can do. The world's problems are too overwhelming. We are blocked by hopelessness, powerlessness and resignation.

Humanity's current story is not a powerful narrative for having the world work. It doesn't empower us with optimism. It doesn't cause us to engage the major sufferings and solve them. It gives us no sense that we're moving in the right direction with a momentum that's growing and expanding. The current story has run its course. It's tired and ineffective. It must change. It can change.

Hope lies in creating a new story of what it means to be a human and what it means to be humanity − of what it means to be an individual and what it means to be the human family.

We need a new narrative that touches our souls and engages us to participate in creating the kind of world we long for. We need a new vision that unleashes what we already know deep within our souls about the kind of world we want, a vision that helps unleash our optimism and energy, and that supports us in taking the steps to make our vision for our world real.

At present, we know how to create hells on earth. Why not create its opposite? Why not have 'We're co-creating Heaven on Earth' as our new story? And there's no need to wait. We can start right now. It's easy to begin. Just answer the *three 'Heaven on Earth' questions:*

1. Recall a time when you experienced Heaven on Earth. What was happening?

2. Imagine you have a magic wand and with it you can create Heaven on Earth. What is Heaven on Earth for you?

3. What simple, easy, concrete step will you take in the next 24 hours to make Heaven on Earth real?

I've asked thousands of people these three questions, and I've observed several very interesting patterns in their answers.

First, people do not ask me to explain what I mean by 'Heaven on Earth'. Instead, they immediately tell me the time or times when they've experienced it. They instinctively know what it is.

The ease of answering the first question tells me that there already exists within us a template, a reference point, a built-in standard by which we know what Heaven on Earth is. We then search for the experiences in our lives that match that. It's the 'already knowing' what Heaven on Earth is that is within us. We know. We simply know.

When I then tell people, they have a magic wand and can create Heaven on Earth, what they say Heaven on Earth is and how they say it is profound. People are still and peaceful when they answer. There is an experience I feel from them of truth, clarity, immediacy and genuineness. I feel they're sharing their Divine essence.

After answering the 3 Heaven on Earth questions, ask three other people (friends, family, colleagues at work) and watch what happens.

Answering the questions begins the process of creating Heaven on Earth. By engaging people, we help open a new, fresh, view of the world. That world becomes full of opportunities and brimming with possibility. And into this new human story, Heaven on Earth, we're invited to creatively contribute the difference that only we can make.

The new story of Heaven on Earth provides the context and then the individual, you, creates the content.

To the sceptics who ask: "What about those for whom Heaven on Earth would be eliminating a particular race or religion, or profiting by polluting the environment?" Those people are the minority, a very small minority. Unfortunately, they're often the people who have an oversized impact on the world's agenda. NO MORE! It's now time for the vast majority of people in the world who want a good and decent and working world to be in charge of building our new human story.

Historically, people seek to impose their view: "Follow my way and it will all work." Imposing a vision never works because it removes the freedom to choose. The vision of creating Heaven on Earth is different in a very significant way. It doesn't impose, it evokes. It evokes the global vision that already lives within each of us.

People do know the kind of world they want, but they're overwhelmed at the thought of making it happen, or embarrassed at what people might say if they talk about it. Once people are given the opportunity to discover their own truth about the kind of world they want and feel free to talk about it, a powerful transformation occurs. A part of themselves they've always known, but haven't met, is revealed. And once this evoked vision of Heaven on Earth is unleashed, a simple, powerful and effective creativity emerges that begins positively impacting the world.

We are beginning to have the kind of world we long for. We can begin living a new story of what it means to be a human and what it means to be humanity. We are creating Heaven on Earth.

MARTIN RUTTE

Martin Rutte is an international speaker and consultant, and president of Livelihood, a Santa Fe, NM, USA consulting firm. The company's areas of service include strategic vision, creative leadership and dialogue.

Martin has helped formulate and implement strategic visions for senior management teams at many of North America's leading corporations including, Sony Pictures Entertainment, Southern California Edison, and Esso Petroleum. He has addressed the Corporate Leadership & Ethics Forum of the Harvard Business School four times.

He is co-author of the New York Times Business bestseller, *Chicken Soup for the Soul at Work*. His newest book is *Project Heaven on Earth: The 3 simple questions that will help you change the world ... easily.* It empowers the reader to engage in creating Heaven on Earth, the new story of what it means to be a human and what it means to be humanity.

www.projectheavenonearth.com

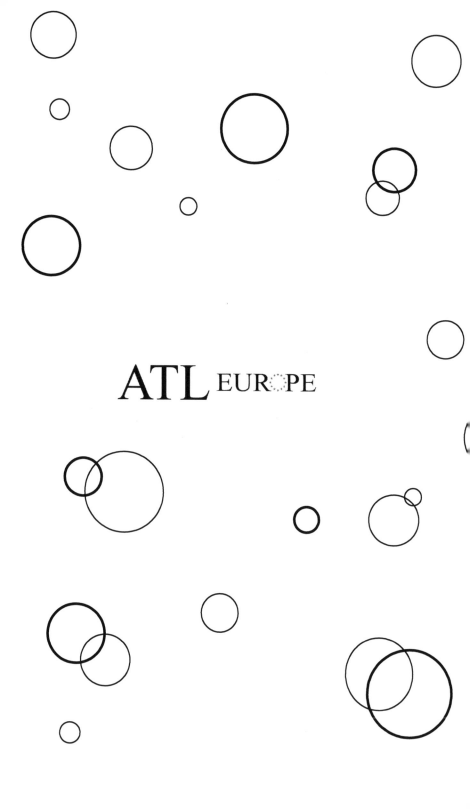

Chapter 34

THE ART OF THE SEVEN ARTS

Marinella Setti

Do you like films? Or even if you don't, I'm sure you must have a favourite film, or even a few favourite films? But just the one will do for now: think about your favourite movie, and ask yourself this question: "What is it about this movie I like so much?" I have a few favourite films, but if I had to choose one it would be Alfred Hitchcock's *Vertigo*.

And if I ask myself the question I am posing to you, here's what I would say: "This film inspires me, excites me, presents me with a spiritual bridge between visual dimensions and shows me a great artist at the top his game. But I also love *Groundhog Day*, which for all purposes is not considered an art movie, and yet my reasons for liking it would be similar."

Because I am a filmmaker, movies are my art of choice, and they have the power to shape consciousness. Which is why I asked you why your favourite movie *is* your favourite movie. What is it that you're left with after you've watched it, or even during it? Is your life any different afterwards, even for a moment? You may feel inspired, so more life was breathed into the life you already have. Is it as if you had inhaled air many times and very fast and the extra oxygen started to open new neural pathways and new synapses formed in your brain? I am putting into words the feeling I have after watching a favourite film, or a new film which might also have that impact.

I have also had this feeling looking at paintings by Van Gogh and Caspar David Friedrich. It is a physical ontological sensation. It is as if the artist's soul has been encapsulated in that object or few frames of film, like a white 'horcrux' (to quote JK Rowling), and my communion with it is what opens it. Film is spiritual and ontological communication; it is the synthesis of spatial and temporal arts, and it's not surprising it is called the seventh art (the other six are architecture, sculpture, painting, music, dance and poetry).

I am a filmmaker, but I was an artist before I knew what art is. But even if I knew, I would not have called myself as such: my grandfather Orlando liked to call himself a craftsman, when in fact, by today's standards, he was a true artist. He was raised by strict Italian parents; whose *ethos* was hard work and the rewards it brings. He was sent to Milan to study textile design, and returned to his father's factory where he became its chief designer. I remember growing up watching him draw, design, create wire machines, toy animals made out of stale bread and toothpicks, and stencil papercuts of all sizes.

And yet he refused to be called an artist. It could have been the way he was raised, to consider artists as people who idle away with a brush and have no goal in life. If I think about all the great painters or filmmakers I admire and read about their lives, there is a common thread about them: they were searching for something intangible, like a fine tuning of an antenna. Van Gogh wrote to his brother Theo: "One must work long and hard to arrive at the truthful," so maybe his notion of artists wasn't so different from my grandfather's, although Van Gogh was quite proud to call himself an artist. His paintings hang in museums worldwide, and people flock to see them. With films, *It's A Wonderful Life*, which was made in the early 1940s, is to this day the most-loved Christmas film ever. Why? Because these works contain the essence of the human condition in its transient flesh and blood passage through earth. And this stuff resonates with most people.

What is art and what impact does it have in your life? You may like to bake cakes or create clothes, or go to pottery or dance lessons, but at the same time not consider yourself an artist as such. You don't have canvases or statues hanging from galleries or museums, so perhaps you think it's not really for you. But art is, fundamentally, the act of manifesting being in the world and communicating that being to others.

Art is an access to the eternal, or rather it translates the eternal into a dialogue in the world. But that's what I say. If you create something in the world, something that takes you out of time and space concerns, what would you call it? Maybe calling something art is what keeps you from doing it? I am inviting you to step out of a comfort zone of 'I can't really draw,' or 'I can't sing or dance,' and embrace the expression gifted to you at birth. Perhaps, like my granddad, you are really good at some things, but never gave much thought to it.

Ultimately, it doesn't matter whether what you do is art or not, because no one will be judging you on it. Well, maybe they will, because human beings are judgmental, but who cares? The world will be a lesser place until you let your soul sing from the rooftops.

MARINELLA SETTI

Marinella Setti is a multi-award winning filmmaker and writer, originally from São Paulo, Brazil, and has been a UK resident since 1995.

Having built a previous career as a graphic designer, drummer and singer in pop bands, she realised that filmmaking was her one true calling outside her home country. Lacking the funds to study filmmaking, she split her time between working as a volunteer for National Film & TV graduation projects and being a macrobiotic chef at the East West restaurant in east London.

She took the personal development course *Landmark Forum* in 2001, which prompted her to create her own film projects. Since 2004, she has directed two short films and one medium-length film, and is preparing to direct her first feature film in north Wales in 2018.

Marinella will publish her first book through Balboa Press, a division of Hay House.

www.marinellasetti.com
twitter.com/marinellasetti
www.instagram.com/marinellasetti
www.facebook.com/marinella.setti

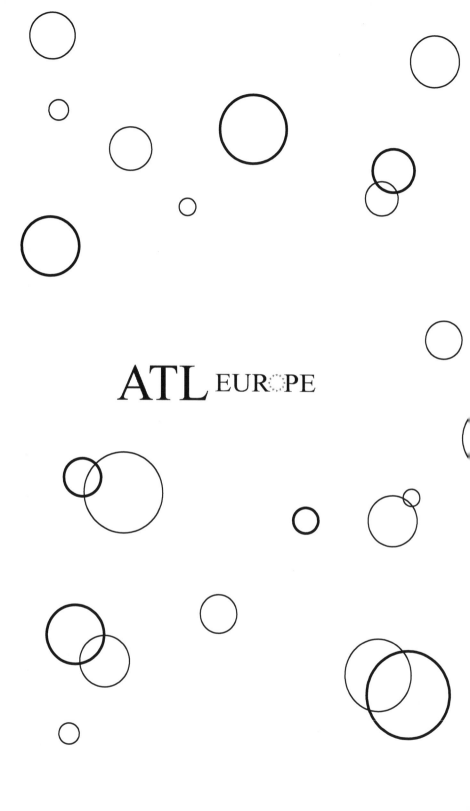

Chapter 35

THE SECRET LANGUAGE OF YOUR SYMPTOMS

Louise K Shaw

Have you ever been in so much pain, you'd do anything for it to stop? It's July 2008 and the clinical coolness of the room I find myself in, is in stark contrast to the blazing heatwave outside in Beverly Hills, California. I'm nervously playing with the piece of paper on my lap, rolling it up into a tight tube, then opening it again to scan the words once more. The door opens and he walks in with a huge envelope in his hands and a stern look across his face. He catches my eye but my stomach churns as I feel the insincerity of his forced smile.

"Well, Ms Shaw, it's as I suspected. The X-ray clearly shows the damage and I'm afraid surgery is the only option to stop the pain and enable you to walk properly again."

Your body is a library for your stories

The first seven years of a child's life are crucial to the development of their personality and it's during this time that many of their beliefs are formed. This is because they're highly suggestible to what's going on around them, what they're hearing, feeling and seeing, as they've developed the use only of beta and theta brainwaves. These are the same brainwaves accessed through meditation and hypnosis and result in a 'super learning state'. It's during this time that you would have formed many beliefs about yourself and the world around you.

Simply put, beliefs are opinions and quite often we live our lives based on other people's opinions. Think about what you believe because your parents or primary caregivers did? Does it hold true for you now? People even hold on to beliefs when they no longer support them or they have outgrown them, which would be like believing in Father Christmas as an adult. Yet many people still tell themselves they're not good enough, attractive enough, intelligent enough, even though they first heard this when they were a child. Over time these beliefs become elaborate stories as events in our life provide evidence to affirm the initial belief.

The divorce provides proof that you're not really loveable or good enough. The redundancy proves you're not intelligent enough. The life-altering diagnosis confirms your belief that bad things always happen to you. Now obviously you aren't aware you're doing this, because the most damaging beliefs are the ones operated by your subconscious mind, the mind operating on autopilot and through habit.

Back to the future

After a year of visiting chiropractors to ease the debilitating pain I was in, I'd finally had enough. Nothing was working and I found it difficult to concentrate as a result of the numerous painkillers I was taking throughout the day. The specialist advised that an 8mm herniated disc was pressing against my sciatic nerve, and his solution was to remove the disc from my spine.

Pills and surgery are the typical solutions to health concerns in the western world, although not necessarily from choice, rather more from familiarity. After all, it has its roots set in a perspective that was established by Sir Isaac Newton, over 300 years ago. He proposed that we are mechanical entities and if we experience any symptoms, then this means the body is being attacked by something outside its control, or it has stopped working properly.

When I left the hospital, I was determined to find another way, although I had no idea how the damage in my back was going to be healed without surgery. My gut feeling started me on a journey to find an alternative solution and a year later, I found it. More importantly, within five days of experimenting with this technique, I was walking properly, the painkillers were in the bin and no scalpel had touched a hair on my body.

I discovered that my thoughts about past events were creating my symptoms. When I was able to change these thoughts, and the associated emotions, the pain disappeared. The experience of healing myself from physical pain, and later from severe emotional pain, has enabled me to support many people to learn the secret language of their symptoms to discover what's really causing them.

Your body is an intelligent organism made up of energy, something the ancient civilisations knew about. In fact, Hippocrates said, long before the birth of Christ: "Natural forces within us are the true healers of disease." It's imperative for the future of our health to elaborate on the knowledge that's been around for centuries: one that focuses on empowering, not disempowering people.

The duality of disconnection

Most people don't see the connection between events in their past, their beliefs, emotions and their symptoms, especially if these are in the body. If you've experienced traumatic events in your past, the emotional impact of each event creates an energy surge in your body. If you aren't able to release this energy, your body has to create a way of doing it. Imagine your body is like a pressure cooker and your emotions are the steam. If you put the lid on the pot (in other words, you continually ignore your emotions relating to events in the past or you haven't made peace with them), sooner or later the lid will explode off. In the same way, your body will create symptoms to get your attention to address these events, which is what my body did.

People are so disconnected from what is really happening in their bodies and believe that their health issues can only be solved using pills or surgery. Yet these approaches only mask what is really causing the symptoms. Creating happiness, health and abundance can happen only when you disconnect from a reliance on things outside yourself and truly connect once again to the wisdom held within your body (the natural forces Hippocrates referred to).

Once you achieve this, you'll experience true, long-lasting health and you'll live in an empowered state of being to create the life of your dreams.

LOUISE K SHAW

Louise K Shaw is an international speaker and bestselling author, an experienced energy psychologist and intuitive coach specialising in reconnecting people to the wisdom and healing powers within their body.

You may need help to get back on your feet as a result of health concerns; support to manage the traumatic impact of a life event; or you may be searching for your purpose in life. Where you are in your personal journey will determine what support will have the greatest impact for you right now.

It is also her passion to raise awareness of the biological cause of depression and to inspire those who suffer with the symptoms to regain control of their lives.

Louise's approach enables her clients to find the answers by tapping into the intelligence of their body. Her *Awaken Your Mojo®* series includes group and online coaching programmes and she works individually with private clients.

www.louisekshaw.com
www.facebook.com/mybodywhisperer
www.linkedin.com/in/louisekshaw/

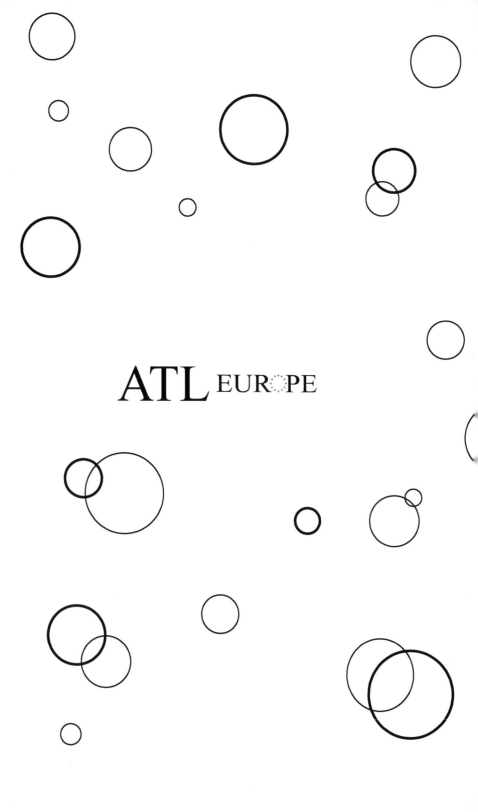

Chapter 36

INNER PEACE IS YOUR TRUTH

Milica Stojiljković

Let me tell you a story about two medical students. You may have already found it somewhere near you. Or perhaps you have participated in this actual event.

The first student I will talk about was a proud member of a family that had raised generations of successful medical doctors. The second was a common young man from a small town, whose parents knew nearly nothing about medicine. The demanding future profession they had chosen made them pass the initial exams with flying colours.

However, the first student gradually started to trade on his family's reputation, boasting about his ancestors' knowledge and experience, although he was still far from attaining such knowledge and experience. He already had clear plans about his medical specialty and the place where he would be a resident doctor. Wherever he went, his boasting echoed loudly. There were those who adored him and those who envied him.

Personally, he was satisfied with the situation, as he liked the role of a star among peers with similar ambitions. He was so immersed in the self-image he created that he seemed to have forgotten that he should study meticulously for more difficult exams. Study material kept piling up and the carelessness to which he was prone meant that he was losing a battle to meet numerous commitments and deadlines.

One exam after another, he failed them all. He hid growing panic inside him by attending peer parties, where he certainly strived to be the focus of everyone's attention. When failure became regular, he lost control and did not know how to find a way out. He reached a point that needed intervention of medical doctors, his parents' friends.

Meanwhile, the other student worked hard. He spent a certain number of hours poring over books every day, devoted to the idea of becoming a doctor. He did not talk much about his ambitions, as they did not obsess him. It seemed that his patient work would bear the results he wanted. He had several dear friends with whom he spent his leisure time and did not obsess about attending peer parties.

While the first student was acting like a star, he learned the study material, page by page. When he encountered difficulties, he would raise his commitment to a higher level. While the first student failed the exams, he received high grades. While the first one was overwhelmed with panic, he quietly enjoyed the satisfaction of passing the exams. While doctors attempted to cure the first student, he was becoming a doctor.

The story about these two students has reminded me of life choices that we all have. In order to know which choice is the right one for us, first we need to realise who we are. And to get to know oneself, it is necessary to devote time and attention to that process, just like the second student did by gaining knowledge required to pass the exams. Every choice is a new exam for us. Every choice is a kind of noise that we can overcome only by developing inner silence and peace.

When I realised and accepted this, my life started changing drastically. My attention became focused on my inner peace, and the more peace pervaded, the less anxious I felt. Bearing in mind the story about two students, here are three truths about the significance of developing inner peace.

1. Inner peace helps you get to know yourself

Like starting to acquire knowledge about anything by learning basic facts, we cannot become experts in managing our own lives before truly getting to know ourselves. If we listen only to other people and their opinion of us, we strive towards something that sounds good, without checking whether it is good for us, too, and then we might end up like the first student.

On the other hand, if we observe ourselves in silence every day, we start perceiving a focus of our thoughts, our feelings, the state of our body and thus we gain knowledge about ourselves. The second student gradually acquired such knowledge and successfully passed his exams. Simultaneously, by getting to know ourselves, we start understanding that other people have similar virtues and flaws and that helps us understand them better and criticise them less, reducing potential anxiety others may cause to us.

2. Inner peace allows us to feel fullness of our lives

When we develop a peaceful state of mind, we start enjoying beauty at every moment. We become grateful for everything we have, instead of hurting for what we do not have. The first student sought pleasure at peer parties, running away from the actual problem, while the other one was happy with his successful results, even when some lessons were difficult.

3. Inner peace accepts quietly any anxiety that may arise

When we regularly develop a peaceful state of mind, it is completely natural for anxiety to surface occasionally, such as during difficult lessons. Then we know that nature has day and night, cold and warm, and that the same succession comes to our life in the form of new knowledge we need to acquire. Also, we understand that these are not irreconcilable extremes, but correlated parts of the same whole.

The second student understood this well. He spontaneously applied the model of gaining medical knowledge to his own life. Therefore, it is important to intentionally develop our inner peace every day. It will take only 15 minutes to close your eyes, sit comfortably and focus on a peaceful state of mind. It is useful to say quietly: "Let this day be optimised for me."

This meditation will help you develop your inner peace, regardless of external events. If you do not have enough time, and circumstances are stressful, it is useful to stop for 10 seconds and focus on your breathing. That is how we say to anxiety: "Stop!" and allow peace to continue its mission of developing and expressing our inner beauty.

MILICA STOJILJKOVIĆ

Milica Stojiljković is the author of the personal development programme, *I Feel Good* and the founder of the I Feel Good personal development centre in Belgrade, the capital of Serbia.

She is an author, public speaker, meditation teacher and Bach Flower Remedies practitioner. Via lectures, workshops and seminars which she participates in and organises, she motivates individuals and groups to acquire skills and practice of good communication with oneself and with others.

For more than 15 years, she was a communications professional in marketing agencies and companies. For 10 years she has been studying and practising personal development skills, including western science and the long-standing tradition of the East.

She is a literature professor and regularly publishes her work on her website.

www.lepomije.rs
www.facebook.com/lepomije.milicastojiljkovic

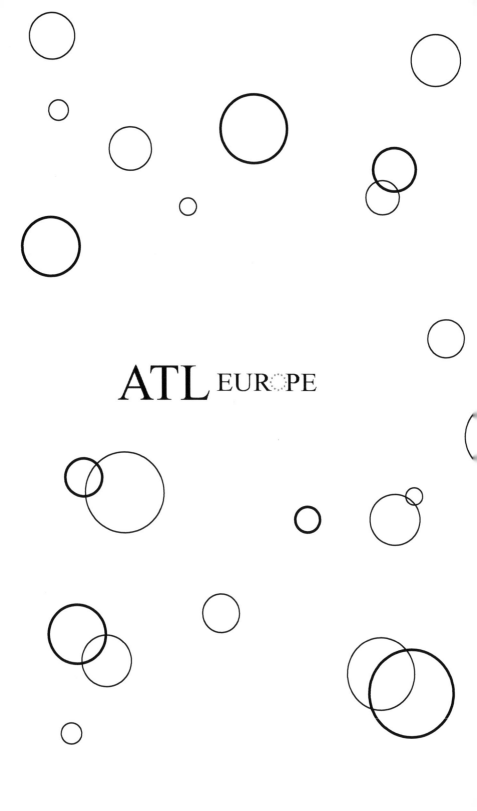

Chapter 37

HAPPINESS IS AN INSIDE JOB

Els Timmerman

It happened one evening during a school excursion in the third year of secondary education. We were staying in a German city with a lovely lake. For the first time in my life I saw a falling star. I spontaneously made a silent wish, which I'd like to share with you this very moment: "I wish to make people happy!"

Now, so many years later, I understand the importance of that moment: I had unknowingly felt my life's mission.

That star was the sign that it was time to start my voyage towards the meaning of happiness. At first, I thought that by making people happy, I myself would find the highest level of happiness. But one of the most important lessons I have learned along the road: we can't create the happiness in other people. You are the only one who can give happiness to yourself.

In my year of specialisation in kinetic therapy, I discovered the principle that body and mind are one. I noticed how one can use the body as a transformation tool to create a change in the mind. I noticed how people blossomed, how their self-confidence increased. I became aware that every creature contains a reason, deep within, why he or she reacts in a certain way on the circumstances which present themselves.

And then I became ready to cross the path of my spiritual teacher, Marie Diamond. And I thought: "Yes, finally!" I ended my old life and room for spirituality came into my life. I learned how to visualise tubes of light: a meditation technique that connects with white, blue, rose and violet light. Being a highly sensitive person, I appreciated these tools as a gift from heaven.

During my childhood days, I usually was overwhelmed like by a gigantic wave of impressions, emotions and thoughts from the outside world. My high sensitivity expressed itself in many questions: "Why do I experience myself as different from my contemporaries? Why do I lose myself (so easily)? Why do I always immediately feel somehow guilty?" By integrating colour meditation in my daily life, I feel more and more my inner strength. So, this is where I found myself: living my life rather than just trying to survive.

Colour meditation

Tube of white light: your own source of strength

First you place white light around you, you immerse yourself in it and this way you get in contact with your own source of strength.

Tube of blue light: protection

By working with blue light, the thoughts and emotions of other people enter less harshly. You perceive the emotions of the other person, without being caught up in the wave of their emotions. I finally could function within a group of people without the feeling of hovering above my own body. Blue brings your thoughts to peace and gives you strength and confidence, you remain with yourself. You develop a deep trust that everything will turn out well in the end.

Tube of rose light: love in all its aspects

Rose light makes you feel as if you lie within a flower and thousands of rose petals encircle you. Rose is the colour of love and support. You feel yourself supported. By placing the rose colour visually all around you, you find the right people on your path to take further steps. Rose also means self-love, and self-esteem. You dare to say no, and you don't want to keep pleasing everyone. Before, I thought: "This way I will make the other person happy!" but finally I was searching only for the approval of others. You draw a boundary out of respect, by which you feel what you really do like. Only now I learned to say fully *yes* to myself.

If in a process of mourning there is something you really need, it is the softness of rose. I discovered this myself with my own daughter, Amarylis.

During my pregnancy, I felt so much love within me, that we gave her the second name 'Love'. Such an immense happiness I felt! When I had to hand back Amarylis, I went deep. That day the woman next door and I would go for a bicycle tour, but when I opened the front door, with bloodshot eyes, I told her: "I really can't make it today." But with all her heart my friend enveloped me with the feeling: let it happen, it is permitted, if it doesn't work, it doesn't work. It's good the way you feel now. It became a beautiful bicycle tour while tears kept flowing. That day became the turning point in my sorrow. I gave myself permission to let the pain just be. My heart filled itself with tenderness, softness, with … Love.

Tubes of violet light: clean up

Violet cleans your emotions, thoughts and impressions – like some washing powder that you add to the white wash so that the purity of the soul becomes visible. This is the way a seven-year-old child explained it to her mother one day in my practice. Before, when somebody told me something, it remained occupying my thoughts. With violet light, I can solve this. On a deeper level, violet can give me the strength to forgive, and if forgiving is possible, you feel enormously liberated. That which has happened no longer dominates your life and your behaviour. Violet works deeply in the roots of your being, even up to your former lives.

All clear!

Fabulous! What a fabulous change this colour meditation has brought into my life. Colours have their own energy, which influences your mood. You learn to know yourself better, you dare to say no (or willingly say yes) and you understand who you are with your positive and less positive characteristics.

And every day I keep working on this. Look at it as a kind of top sport, in which you bring the discipline to practise every day to grow more powerful. You are the only one who can establish this change, this tuning in on your own happiness. Happiness is definitely an inside job. For me this means that I turn the negative aspects of high sensitivity into a source of strength. My question to you: "How do you give happiness to yourself?"

To discover this for yourself, the colour meditation from this text is a powerful tool. Click on the following link: https://www.lightness.be/atl

ELS TIMMERMAN

Els Timmerman is a certified transformational leader. She is a licentiate in kinesiotherapy and attended the specialised course 'kritische ontwikkelingsbegeleiding method Hendrickx' about the cooperation between body and mind.

With Marie Diamond, she developed her spiritual sensitivity and learned transformation. She followed Lu Jong and Tog Chöd by Rinpoche Tulku Lobsang and passes this on in weekly workshops.

In her readings, workshops and courses, she inspires people who are interested in transformation, the universal laws and self-development. You can contact her in her practice for personal coaching, where she supports people in their quest for happiness. At the moment, she is working on a course to help people become conscious of their own strength.

She is the mother of three children: Amarylis (+), Tiebe and Xian. She lives with her husband and children in the fields of Moerbrugge, Belgium.

www.lightness.be
www.facebook.com/ Els Lightness
www.instagram.com/els.lightness/

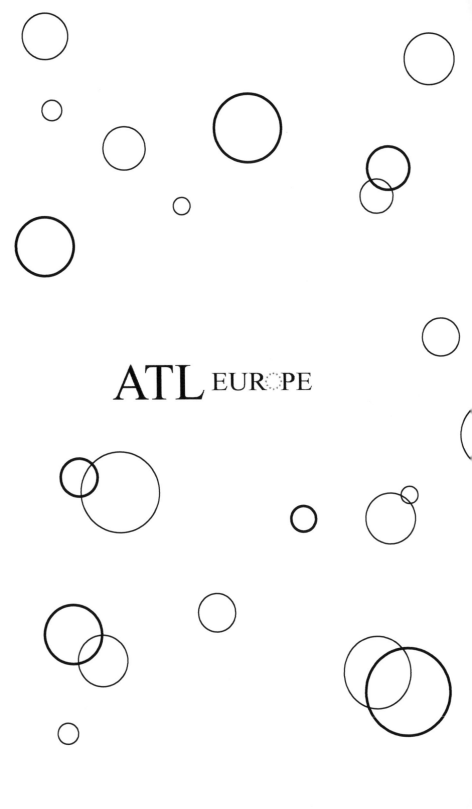

Chapter 38

MIND YOUR HEART

Mimi Van Mileghem

After I had completed a master's degree in religious studies, my head was full of knowledge about religion, spirituality, morality and philosophy. In the 80s and 90s, I co-authored textbooks on moral and spiritual development. I was guiding people towards conscientious decisions. As a dedicated teacher, I liked to be in front of the class well-informed, self-assured, convincing, while others listened. My mind was my guide.

However, I was actually very sensitive. Have you ever heard of someone who can catch a TV-channel and watch it behind her eyelid, without a TV in the room? Well, now you have. It happened many times. The only thing I needed to do was lay down with my head in a certain angle towards my bedroom window. But I depended on my brain to survive the emotional turmoil of life. Faced with spirituality, I tended to run away. Away from sentimentality, wishful thinking, naiveté. Afraid of not being in touch with reality. I had the feeling spiritual people tended to lose their capacity to be perceptive and vigilant. Mind your head, I joked. For me, they walked on thin ice.

Then I took classes in neurolinguistic programming (NLP), which showed me I was in my head most of the time. My mind was my safe haven, and I tried to master my life from there. It became clear how my ego was holding me back from relaxing. Moreover, a deep longing for spiritual experiences came to the surface, no longer buried underneath a pile of objections and fears. Transpersonal

NLP coaching showed me how to start exploring a spiritual dimension to life, but I wanted to go deeper.

Meanwhile I worked hard, had three children and got ill. Due to the weakness of my body, I had to lie down many hours a day for six years. Losing my job, not being able to take care of my children, seeing my husband taking over the household – it was a challenge. But during this time, I had to acknowledge the value of my own coping skills and meditation.

Blessed is the woman who referred me to Marie Diamond! Marie was so calm, smart and down to earth that I gave her a chance, although in a cautious way. In 1995, I took the first of her Inner Diamond Meditation courses. These techniques were so to the point, so safe and efficient. It was astonishing. They opened up a whole new world of creativity and wisdom. My clairvoyance developed.

From the first few days, I was able to receive information, whole scenes of people's lives – with their consent. My intuition and telepathy evolved during the years, from deep comprehension to the capacity to merge, to become one with bodies, thoughts, objects, atmospheres. For instance, connected in meditation with someone's liver, I found myself blown up, obstructing a channel of the liver, for instance. Not only could I see the problem: I became the blockage.

Additionally, these techniques teach you how to work with the spiritual level beyond the soul, and to do energetic transformations at the deepest level. The possibilities are beyond imagination. I finally learned to surrender, to let go control and master my susceptibility. Nevertheless, it took 10 years before all my detailed questions and suspicions were addressed. Since 2005, I have led practical spiritual courses as an Inner Diamond Meditation master teacher, delivering Marie Diamond's strategy to enlightenment.

Because of these years of experience, I became absolutely sure we have a sixth sense to gather information, next to our brain and the five senses. It would be such a valuable asset for the academic world to embrace this capacity. That's where I am aiming for in Project Kernkracht, an initiative of Professor Emeritus Van de Kerckhove, stimulating an openness in academic environment towards the energetic dimension of reality.

I went back to work, and I implemented what I had learned. In 2004 my husband and I established our own ethics consultancy, Essentie. We help governmental and social care organisations to take care of their integrity policies. Our specialty is training them in judging morally, choosing the right thing to do, for example: "Shall I do what is ordered or follow my own point of view in this?"

When we go into a company, we ask them how they usually know they have taken a morally right decision, and guide them to a description of what morally right actually is. Thus, they have a shared moral compass. Then we identify an issue, one of their real problems and look at the stakeholders, options and arguments. We lead them through an objective and effective inquiry towards a prudent judgment, ensuring the rights and interests of everyone involved are taken into account. The method can also be used to investigate the moral quality of decisions already made. During the process, I explore the value of the intuition in the search for the best solution, in accordance with their company ethos.

Nowadays we encounter more and more leaders and employees who possess highly evolved intuition. It is a challenging situation for them. They wonder: "How do we have efficient meetings and shared decisions when information is gained by intuition? Especially when we are surrounded by supervisors or colleagues who do not know or trust it?" Furthermore, higher intuition might be a valuable source of information, but following your intuition is not a guarantee for a morally right decision. A more instinctive intuition isn't as meaningful as an insight from yourself beyond your ego. Developing intuition is a challenging journey with many conditions and pitfalls – as many pitfalls as the mind has.

Rational thinking and higher intuition are two capabilities that can work together in moral judgment and coaching. The mind can support the intuition by investigating the quality of the insights, with a rational weighing of arguments, and with a conscious choice for justice and equality. Intuition can support the mind. It can introduce extra information, a wider view, an experienced, heartfelt compassion. The heart inspires, the mind inquires.

Integrity is often described as a consistency in thoughts, feelings and actions. However, in my opinion, integrity not only means having an alignment on a psychological level but also on a spiritual level. The highest form of integrity is to be in contact with your heart, your deepest core, beyond ego and the soul. You live from an experienced peace, wisdom and compassion, and wisely reflect on it, too.

Mind your heart.

MIMI VAN MILEGHEM

Mimi Van Mileghem was born in 1960 and studied religious science and philosophy at the University of Leuven.

She has co-authored textbooks and workbooks for counsellors on assertiveness and moral and spiritual development. Her aim is to strengthen individuals and groups in their moral and spiritual integrity, in contact with their essence.

She has developed workshops, seminars and training courses with efficient techniques to enhance moral and spiritual leadership. She is active as an integrity counsellor and trainer in governmental and social care organisations, as a transpersonal NLP coach and a spiritual therapist.

Combining ethical decision-making with intuition is her strength. As an Inner Diamond Meditations master teacher, she has been teaching Marie Diamond's strategy to enlightenment since 2005.

Mimi is a founding member of ATL Europe, and of Project Kernkracht, an initiative of Professor Emeritus J Van de Kerckhove, to stimulate an openness in academic environments towards the energetic dimension of reality. Mimi is a dedicated author, speaker, coach and trainer.

www.essentie.info/en
www.linkedin.com/in/mimi-van-mileghem-a714a544

TRANSFORMATION LESSONS

Get Inspired to Transform Your Life
38 Insights to Manifest Your Best Life

The stories from 38 transformational leaders will inspire you to change your Life. They share with you personal experiences that transformed their lives. Every one of the contributing authors has gone through a transformational experience that helped them on their way to become who they are now. We hope that their stories, their lessons, insights, tools and techniques they share here will support you in your own life.

Author

ATL Europe is a non-profit membership organisation for transformational leaders, speakers, authors, movers and shakers, created in 2012 by Marie Diamond. It is a heart-based community of transformational leaders seeking to bring about an enlightened Europe. Transformational leaders who live and work in Europe come together to support each other in their personal transformational journey, to network and encourage each other's positive impact in Europe and beyond.

Contributing members:

Ania Jeffries

Bea Benkova

Bindar Dosanjh

Carole Fossey

Caroline Laschkolnig

Catherine Edsell

Dr Cheryl Chapman

Els Timmerman

Enya Demeyer

Garry Jones

Dr Gill Barham

Ivan Faes

Ivana Plechinger

Izabella Niewiadomska

Jacinta Murray

Jan Polak

Judith Quin

Kezia Luckett

Liz Keaney

Louise K Shaw

Malou Laureys

Marie Diamond

Marinella Setti

Dr Marion Bevington (Hon)

Martin Laschkolnig

Martin Rutte

Milica Stojiljković

Milijana de Mori

Mimi Van Mileghem

Mindy Gibbins-Klein

Miranda Christopher

Monika Laschkolnig

Nikolina Balenović Knez

Patrick Pype

Sandra Deakin

Sanja Plavljanić-Širola

Tineke Rensen

Viola Edward

Notes:

Notes:

_____

_____

_____

_____

_____

_____

_____

_____

_____

_____

_____

_____

_____

_____

_____

_____

_____

Notes:

Notes:

_____

_____

_____

_____

_____

_____

_____

_____

_____

_____

_____

_____

_____

_____

_____

_____

Notes:

Notes:

Notes: